MW00993853

FabJob G

Become a Personal Concierge

JENNIFER JAMES

FABJOB® GUIDE TO BECOME A PERSONAL CONCIERGE
by Jennifer James

ISBN: 978-1-897286-22-7

Copyright Notice: This edition copyright © 2012 by FabJob Inc. All rights reserved. No part of this work may be reproduced or distributed in any form or by any means (including photocopying, recording, online or email) without the written permission of the publisher. (First edition copyright © 2007 by FabJob Inc.)

Library and Archives Canada Cataloguing in Publication

James, Jennifer, 1975-
FabJob guide to become a personal concierge business
owner / by Jennifer James.

Accompanied by a CD.
Also available in electronic format.
ISBN 978-1-897286-22-7

1. Personal concierges--Vocational guidance. I. FabJob
II. Title.

HD9999.P3942J34 2008   640   C2008-904186-0

Important Disclaimer: Although every effort has been made to ensure this guide is free from errors, this publication is sold with the understanding that the authors, editors, and publisher are not responsible for the results of any action taken on the basis of information in this work, nor for any errors or omissions. The publishers, and the authors and editors, expressly disclaim all and any liability to any person, whether a purchaser of this publication or not, in respect of anything and of the consequences of anything done or omitted to be done by any such person in reliance, whether whole or partial, upon the whole or any part of the contents of this publication. If expert advice is required, services of a competent professional person should be sought.

About the Websites Mentioned in this Guide: Although we aim to provide the information you need within the guide, we have also included a number of websites because readers have told us they appreciate knowing about sources of additional information. (**TIP:** Don't include a period at the end of a web address when you type it into your browser.) Due to the constant development of the Internet, websites can change. Any websites mentioned in this guide are included for the convenience of readers only. We are not responsible for the content of any sites except FabJob.com.

FabJob Inc.
19 Horizon View Court
Calgary, Alberta, Canada T3Z 3M5

FabJob Inc.
4616 25th Avenue NE, #224
Seattle, Washington, USA 98105

To order books in bulk, phone 403-949-2039
To arrange a media interview, phone 403-949-4980

www.FabJob.com
THE DREAM CAREER EXPERTS

Contents

About the Author

 Guide author Jennifer James ran her own part-time personal concierge service for two years, specializing in the specific needs of busy entrepreneurs. From preparing courier packages, to wrapping Christmas gifts, to computer troubleshooting, to drafting letters to her client's lawyers, she did it all… with a smile!

She switched gears to help launch the editorial department at FabJob Inc., the world's leading publisher of information about dream careers. She has edited, researched for, and contributed to more than 40 FabJob career guides, including the *FabJob Guide to Become a Professional Organizer* and *FabJob Guide to Become a Party Planner*, as well as the bestseller *Dream Careers*. For this guide she interviewed successful personal concierges, and she adds her own entrepreneurial expertise.

Acknowledgements

Thank you to the following concierge business owners and experts for sharing their advice and experience in this guide:

- *Jill Burstein*
  Jill will… Concierge Service, Detroit, MI

- *Elyse Coleman*
  Life/Time CEO Services, Lincoln, DE
  http://wecreatetime.com

- *Delmar Johnson*
  The Concierge Place, Raleigh, NC

- *Bev Riggins*
  Midwest Concierge Service, Central Illinois

- *Dustyn Shroff*
  One Concierge, West Palm Beach, FL
  www.oneconcierge.com

1. Introduction

1.1 The World of the Personal Concierge

Do you love to feel needed and appreciated? Are you a true "people person" with boundless energy? Are you known in your circle of friends as the one with all the answers, or who always saves the day? Do you get your greatest happiness from helping others?

Welcome to the world of the personal concierge — the ultimate helping career. These friendly problem-solvers know how to get anything done, quickly and professionally. They assist busy and wealthy people who are short on time, and who have tasks or projects they need to get done.

Personal concierges do some things hands-on, but they also have a vast network of reliable, trusted connections they can call on anytime. These organized individuals can juggle many tasks at the same time, and they always keep their cool. If this sounds like you, read on to discover how you can earn a great living running your own personal concierge service.

1.1.1 What a Personal Concierge Does

A personal concierge takes on any tasks that their clients are too busy to get done themselves, such as grocery shopping, running errands, or getting the car serviced. They generally charge a rate of anywhere from $15 to $85 an hour, depending on the local market and the services requested.

Just 15 years ago, concierges were simply the gatekeepers and service people associated with expensive hotels and posh apartment buildings. But today it's not just the extremely wealthy who have a need for occasional assistance with day-to-day living. Everyone from dual-income families to single parents to traveling executives can be totally time-strapped, and willing to pay for what is known as "lifestyle management."

Personal concierges are not butlers, nannies, or housekeepers; yet they may help their clients locate these services. Unlike personal assistants, who often work for only one person and may even be available to them 24 hours a day, personal concierges service a number of clients for a few hours a week. Unlike executive assistants, a personal concierge deals less with office work, and more with helping manage personal lives.

Are you the type of person who gets bored by routine? Well as a personal concierge, you'll never have two days exactly the same. Things you may do or arrange for clients include (but are far from limited to) the following, all of which are covered in this guide:

- Grocery shopping

- Buying gifts

- Planning trips and booking travel

- Obtaining concert and event tickets

- House-sitting

- Occasional pet care

- Planning dinner parties and other gatherings

- Finding and hiring reliable contractors

- Getting cars serviced

- Delivery and pick-up services

- Assistance in relocating to a new town or city

- Handling mini-emergencies

Since every client will have his or her own unique to-do list, the types of services that personal concierges offer are quite varied. The touchstone used in the industry is that if the request is illegal or immoral, the concierge will not oblige. Otherwise, it's "anything goes," and the best personal concierges are known for their resourcefulness, as well as their commitment to clients' privacy.

While personal concierges can find full-time work with corporations, hotels, and other companies in competitive industries, this guide focuses on starting your own personal concierge business. This doesn't mean you can't target both individuals and corporations as clients, just that you'll be your own boss, set your own hours, and decide what services you will offer.

1.1.2   The Marketplace Today

Personal concierge is a relatively new career, born out of an ever-growing need for more free time. "A common misconception is that concierge services are too expensive, and that they're only for the rich and famous. Today *everyone* is busy, overworked, and doesn't have enough time to do even the necessary things on their 'to-do' list," says Delmar Johnson of the Concierge Place.

There's never been a better time to break into this market. Consider that:

- In her book *The Overworked American*, Harvard economist Juliet Schor revealed statistics that showed that in the last twenty years, the amount of time Americans have spent at their jobs has risen steadily.

- The Families and Work Institute reports that more than half of U.S. employees surveyed felt "overworked at least sometimes" in the last three months.

- According to a recent survey by Salary.com and America Online, employees waste about twice as much time at work as their employers think. Running errands outside the office accounted for 7.6% of this lost productivity.

Enter the ultimate time-saving solution: the personal concierge. By the early 21st Century (2002), *Entrepreneur* magazine included concierge and errand-service businesses in their annual list of top-ten start-up ideas. And according to estimates from the International Concierge and Lifestyle Management Association (ICLMA), this type of service has now become a $1 billion industry worldwide.

According to the ICLMA's 2010 industry survey, even in difficult financial times, personal concierge businesses are increasing. With low start-up costs (51.2% of respondents started their own business with $5,000 or less) and quick returns (23.6% saw profits in the first year), a personal concierge business is an ideal start-up in any economic climate.

"Concierges are everywhere now, in hospitals, malls, apartments and condos, colleges, corporations, and on and on. There has been extraordinary growth in this industry and it continues to grow," says industry insider Delmar Johnson.

The Individual Client

Your typical client will have more money than time, and consider time more valuable than money. According to the International Concierge and Errand Association 2006 Industry Future Watch survey of its members, the average client earned anywhere from $50,000 to $500,000 per year, with most (47%) falling in the $100,000 to $500,000 range. The fact that few of the members surveyed had clients over the $1 million per year income bracket may come as a surprise to those new to the profession. Another finding of interest in this survey, which may help you in determining your client base, is that the average age of most clients was between 31 to 45 (about 55%), followed by 46 to 55 year-old clients (35%).

But these clients won't necessarily have the need for a full-time personal assistant. In fact, the most requested services by individual clients were general errands and household management, representing a combined total of about 54%. Single parents with professional careers, two-income families with a combined income of $80,000 or more, wealthy divorced people (usually men) who formerly relied on their spouse to run the household, and busy executives who travel a lot all fall into this category.

You can also choose to target clients who may need concierge services temporarily or on an ongoing basis, such as new mothers, the convalescing, or seniors. Where people used to call a sister, a son, or a grandmother, family networks are not what they used to be, and a personal concierge is the new solution. Other trends working in the favor of personal concierges include more and more people:

- Feeling stressed

- Being overwhelmed with purchasing choices

- Wanting to feel special

- Preferring to choose services based on referrals

- Seeking closer family ties

- Starting their own businesses

- Getting divorced

- Using similar "niche services" like personal chefs and personal shoppers

- Striving to achieve work-life balance

"People have longer commutes, longer work hours, and their kids' schedules are booked solid," confirms personal concierge Jill Burstein. "Many middle-class families have somebody clean their house these days because they understand the value of their time. Oh, and the gas costs! [Hiring a personal concierge] will become very commonplace once people see that it is cost-effective."

Of course, some concierge businesses do have celebrity clients. This can be anyone who is a television or film star, stage actor, author, sports star, musician, politician, and so on. Even business executives can be celebrities (think Bill Gates or Donald Trump), so this type of client can include a very broad range of people with an equally broad range of needs for personal concierge services. Remember, too, that not all celebrities are

A-listers like Brad Pitt and Angelina Jolie. Many less well-known celebrities also need personal concierge services.

Like your other individual clients, celebrities have a wide range of needs and so require a wide range of services. Whether it's helping them remember birthday gifts, making travel and entertainment arrangements, or running errands, you may become the person a celebrity's personal assistant calls on when certain services are needed.

The Corporate Client

Businesses are also turning to personal concierge services in an effort to attract and retain employees and clients. The Fortune 500 companies started this trend, and now many progressive-minded CEOs are adding what are known as "work-life benefits" to their compensation packages, which include access to a personal concierge service. The "corporate concierge" specializes in providing concierge services to this niche market.

Having a personal concierge available saves employees from taking time off work to run personal errands, and allows them to more fully enjoy their time off. The effective impact on productivity (and reduced stress levels) is a no-brainer. Condominiums, office buildings and membership groups are also seeing the value of adding concierge services to their list of amenities, in an effort to attract members, tenants, or buyers.

While the best corporate markets are in cities with booming economies, any business with a branch near you may require someone local. Your location may lead you to target clients based on local industries, such as filmmaking or high-tech. Because the personal concierge is such a new concept, there are no hard and fast rules. You are free to take your business in any direction you believe there is a market for. In this guide you will learn how to market concierge services to both individuals and corporate clients.

1.1.3   Benefits of this Career

"I just like helping make life easier for people. I also like the thrill of the hunt. So if I am asked to find something, I am just tickled to death when I do. I like

giving some folks a sense of independence, and easing the time burden for others."

> — Jill Burstein, personal concierge

The benefits of a career as a personal concierge are tremendous. In addition to the "cool factor" of working in a new and exciting industry, rubbing elbows with wealthy or powerful clients, and getting treated like a high roller yourself on occasion, here are some of the benefits most commonly associated with this profession.

Flexibility

As a personal concierge you can work from home, scheduling your errands and other work around family life or other commitments. In emergencies you may need to respond to clients quickly, and sometimes you'll have deadlines that require long days. But a career as a personal concierge definitely offers more flexibility than most.

Helping People

How can a powerful executive who makes decisions all day long not know what she wants to give her mother for a birthday gift? It happens, and you are the one who can step in and help. "The most rewarding parts of the job are the relationships with clients I have formed," says Bev Riggins of Midwest Concierge Service.

More than once in this career you'll hear clients tell you that you worked a miracle, that you saved the day, and that they don't know what they would do without you. According to CEO of One Concierge Dustyn Shroff, "on a daily basis, I can truly say that I make peoples' plans and dreams turn into a reality." You will be trusted and appreciated by your loyal clients, and you will see firsthand the difference you make. You will give couples and families time to spend with each other. Your helping hand and gift of time, albeit indirectly, may save marriages, let children feel loved and important, and even save lives by reducing stress.

Great Income Potential

Personal concierges charge hourly rates of anywhere from $15 to $85 an hour, and sometimes more. Corporate concierges charge additional fees per employee, and you can earn bonus income through commissions and referral fees from vendors. Once your business is well established you can expect gross revenues of $50,000 to $100,000 annually, and if you hire employees and open additional locations, earnings exceeding $1 million are the established precedent.

You Can Start Right Now

Working as a personal concierge does not require special training or certification. Instead, you'll build on skills you already have. Like other service businesses, your start-up costs are minimal compared to other businesses. You can work from home, and if you have access to your own computer and cell phone, you already have the equipment you need to get started.

1.2 Inside This Guide

The *FabJob Guide to Become a Personal Concierge* is designed to help you launch into your new career by providing industry information, how-to guidelines, helpful hints on finding clients, and advice on starting your own personal concierge service. It will teach you how to take your natural talents of household management and organization, and turn them into a real way to make money.

Following this brief introduction, Chapter 2 goes over *How to Be a Personal Concierge*, breaking down the main tasks you are likely to perform in this career. From shopping, to running errands, to planning parties, to booking contractors, to booking travel, to helping people move to a new town or city, this section has you covered with helpful hints and insider advice.

Chapter 3 (*Developing Your Skills*) is all about those important first steps of preparation: discovering the common skills needed in this business, developing your own skills through research and experience, and considering the schools available if you decide to further your education before setting out on your new career.

Chapter 4 leads you through all the steps necessary in *Starting a Concierge Business*: figuring out how much money you'll need on start up, writing a business plan, choosing a name, and getting legal matters like insurance and business registration arranged. This chapter also includes important information you'll need for setting up your office, keeping track of your business finances, and a look at the subject of franchises.

Chapter 5 (*Running a Personal Concierge Business*) helps you refine your business concept, and figure out how you will operate from day to day. It explains how to do a client consultation, what to include in your contract, and different models for setting your fees (with some real-life examples). It also tells you how to set up strategic partners with vendors and other service providers, how to hire help when you need it, and gives you on-the-job strategies for success.

Chapter 6 (*Getting Personal Concierge Clients*) sets you up to land that first client, with techniques to evaluate the local market, choose a niche, and select the services you'll offer. The section also covers developing your website and other marketing tools, three proven ways to use publicity to boost awareness of your business, referrals and word of mouth, networking, and how to target and approach the corporate clients in your area.

The guide concludes with some words of inspiration and a handy list of websites you can use to continue your research. Throughout the guide you will find samples and questionnaires you can adapt for your business, as well as encouragement and ideas from a number of working personal concierges who have kindly shared their advice and experience with you.

The information, resources and advice offered on these pages will save you hundreds of hours of research, so that you can start earning money more quickly. You'll avoid the common pitfalls, and make business decisions like an expert. Get ready, because armed with the inside knowledge this guide provides, you could be landing your first client in a very short time from right now!

2. How to Be a Personal Concierge

As the owner of a personal concierge business, you have the choice of working hands-on, providing personal services yourself, or you could manage other service providers to offer personal services through your concierge business.

This chapter offers an introduction to a variety of concierge services you might choose to offer through your business. You can learn more about these services from the resources listed at the end of this guide.

TIP: Before deciding whether to offer a particular service, it is recommended that you read through this entire guide for additional information. For example, if there's a service you would like to offer which you would rather not do yourself, section 5.3 explains how you can find reputable individuals and companies to provide that service through your business.

2.1 Personal/Domestic Services

When people are very busy with work or social activities, their domestic tasks and errands are usually the first things to be put off. Why? Because they are generally tedious and time-consuming, and the list gets so long that it seems pointless to start. You can rescue your clients by taking their to-do lists off their hands. Here are some ways to help.

2.1.1 Running Errands

For many people running errands is time-consuming. They can be stuck in traffic and have trouble finding parking spots. The overwhelming size of box stores and department stores makes it difficult to find the item they need. On-floor staff is often scarce, and line-ups long. Then it's back into the car and back into traffic to get to the next location. No wonder people want to hand off their errand list!

Think of the typical errands that consume your own day: going to the post office, banking or paying bills, picking up prescriptions, visiting specialty shops, getting the dry cleaning dropped off and picked up… these are the same tasks you will take on as a personal concierge, only for someone else.

Your clients will ask you to run errands that could take you all over the city, or out of town. Personal concierge Jill Burstein remembers one of her more unusual requests:

"I was almost home and it was rush hour, when a pregnant mom called me. She was stuck at home with a toddler, and she was craving French onion soup. You know, with the cheese melted on top?

"She called from more than 25 miles away. I explained it would really cost a lot as it was an emergency run, and the mileage charge would be high as well. Also, it would take a long time as I had no freeway route available. But she really wanted the soup.

"I called a soup shop called Zoup, who didn't have it that day but said one of their other shops did. They called the other location and arranged for it to be ready when I got there. I picked it up and sped on over. That was some expensive soup!"

The trick to running errands for your clients is to be efficient, and find ways to save time. Perhaps you have scouted out a little-known place to park, or know a quick route there. If you shop at a certain vendor all the time, you can make a map of the aisle layout to use when you are in a rush. You should also plan your daily errand route to make the most efficient use of gas and time. Use a resource like Google Maps at **http://maps.google.com**. Run errands at off-times when you can, to avoid traffic.

Most businesses know that people are time-starved, and look for ways to get you in and out more quickly. See what services you can pre-arrange online or by phone. For example, you can calculate postage and print a shipping label for a package, buy stamps or even arrange to have postage stamps delivered regularly to you or your clients at the U.S. Postal Service website (**www.usps.com**).

Investigate delivery or pickup service with vendors, and carefully weigh the costs versus your gas and time. You'll save time if you do all your work for a particular client in one day, so you aren't going back and forth to their home as often.

Using GPS Navigation

GPS, or Global Positioning Systems, are becoming increasingly common for consumer use. One of the most common uses available to the public is street mapping, something you will find invaluable as a personal concierge running errands for clients.

A GPS sends a signal to a satellite in stationary orbit (i.e. one that's always over the same spot above the earth) and then the satellite sends a signal back to the GPS receiver with the information of the exact longitude and latitude of the receiver on the ground.

Many handheld, or mobile, GPS mapping units are available and are quite affordable. Many are also available with certain cell phones like the BlackBerry that include telephone, Internet, PDA and other capabilities. A mobile GPS will cost you about

---

$100-$400 or around $200 (plus cell phone service) for an all-in-one unit like the BlackBerry. Visit **www.thegpsstore.com**, **www. gpscentral.ca** or your favorite cell phone service provider to see some of the many units available.

Many new cars, SUVs, vans and trucks have GPS available as an option. These units consist of a screen that displays a map of the locality and a voice-operated command system that allows hands-free operation. Some use a CD map database that contains the maps used in the system, although these are not actually GPS units. A drawback to this type of system is that your maps will eventually become outdated and you'll need to purchase an updated map database.

There are also vehicle destination directions services like GM's On Star system, which costs about $300 per year. Using this service, you press a button to tell an operator your destination, who then downloads a route plan, including directions and distance to upcoming streets where you need to turn, to your car's system. If you stray from the route, the system will automatically re-plan the route and get you back on track.

2.1.2   Home Organizing

If your clients are short on time, chances are that they have some challenges in getting organized. Organizers use tried-and-true strategies to help people reduce clutter, create systems, and make their environments more functional. They help people organize their personal lives, homes, and home offices in a way that makes sense to the clients.

Organizing is a frequent request for personal concierges. Offering organizational services can be a good "foot in the door" with potential clients who are reluctant to hire a personal concierge immediately. Once you have met with them and assessed their needs, you can pitch some ongoing services that will make them regular clients. If organizing is not your thing, you'll want to have some professional organizers in your network of contacts to subcontract or refer clients to.

Depending on the size of the project and whether time is an issue, you could offer clients a "one-day fix," then hire help and get the job done within one day. Or you could bill the client hourly and do the organizing project. Then you can source and purchase organizing products, and start your hands-on work. In some cases, clients need ongoing organizing services.

"One of my first clients asked me to do some filing for her. She seemed overwhelmed by this simple task. When I started filing, I realized why. She had multiple folders for the same clients, folders in her inbox and all over her workspace, and a pile of folders with cribbed notes waiting to be updated. I decided it wasn't just filing she needed, it was a whole filing system. I came up with some solutions for her, but I still filed for her each time I came in. Some people are just 'allergic' to administrative tasks," says Jennifer James, guide author and former personal concierge.

The first step in organizing a home is to assess what is working well for the client, and what is not. Typical organizational trouble areas in the home are closets, home offices, kitchens, bathrooms, attics and basements, and garages. You can use a questionnaire or simply ask your client if there are areas of the home they feel need some help. Document the space and the challenges, set out a plan for the organizing solutions you want to implement, and get the plan approved by the client.

To assist you in documenting the space and setting out an organizing plan, you can use the following forms, reproduced from the *FabJob Guide to Become a Professional Organizer*.

TIP: Unless you are a skilled draftsperson, bring a camera with you as well to take a few pictures of each room. You'll be able to check on any details you may have missed in your notes. Ask clients for permission to take "before-and-after" pictures, which you can later use to demonstrate your excellent work — in a portfolio of past projects and on your website. Make this process easier by using a digital camera for easy uploading to your website.

Organizing Plan Form

Objective: What do you want to accomplish?

_____
_____
_____
_____
_____

Tools: What things will you need to help you organize?

_____
_____
_____
_____

Steps: State the steps of the plan. What will you do? When will you do it? How long should it take?

1. _____
   _____
   _____

2. _____
   _____
   _____

3. _____
   _____
   _____

4. _____
   _____
   _____

5. _____
   _____
   _____

Room Analysis Form

1. How does the client use this space?
   _____
   _____
   _____

2. Describe the layout of the room.
   _____
   _____
   _____

3. Sketch the features of the room, including windows, doors, closets, built-in storage, and furniture placement. Sketch changes desired.

4. Describe the current system, if any. Is there any storage furniture you can take advantage of? Describe the existing closet space and built-in storage.
   _____
   _____
   _____

5. List client's current organizational concerns about the room.
   _____
   _____
   _____

6. Describe the client's "best-case scenario" for this space.
   _____
   _____
   _____

How to Complete the Organizing Plan Form

Objective

The objective is the reason or the goal for a plan. For example, "Getting last year's bills organized and filed."

Tools

Tools, in this case, are the things needed to organize the stuff. They can be anything from a filing cabinet to a modular closet system, to a basket.

Steps

Planning with clients tells them what they are going to do first and how. It allows scheduling of the event. For example:

- Get all bills together

- Sort by type

- Sort by date

- Insert in file

- File alphabetically

If the task is large you may have to break it down into smaller, more manageable steps over time.

While it may seem obvious, if you are going to offer organizational services it's extremely important to "walk the walk." This means complete and neat client folders, a tidy car, a solid scheduling system for your own business, and a well-kept appearance.

2.1.3 Repair and Maintenance

Quick, name five repair and maintenance projects you are putting off right now because you don't have the time. Your busy clients will have a list twice as long as yours, and with the right prompting this is a goldmine of business opportunity for the personal concierge. The trick is that you have to anticipate for your clients, and ask for the business.

Vehicles

Vehicle servicing is a big request in this department. In addition to regular maintenance and oil changes, cars need new tires, repairs, emissions testing, and detailing. Who wants to sit around a dusty waiting room while mechanics take their time getting around to looking at the vehicle, only to find out you'll need to drop it off another day? (Answer: you do, for a fee!)

The personal concierge arranges to pick up the vehicle at a time convenient to the client, bring it in to the shop, wait or pick it up later, and deliver it back to the client. In many cases the client simply hands over the keys in the morning at their place of work, and gets them back before the end of the day to drive home.

Vehicle maintenance offers a great opportunity for the personal concierge to pick up monthly or weekly repeat business with a client. Keep records for the client of when (and at what mileage) the vehicle received certain services, and use the car manual to see what services are recommended at what mileage. Don't forget to include your clients' seasonal vehicles on the list, such as RVs, boats, and motorcycles.

Home Repairs and Renovations

Home repair and maintenance is another service offering that will be appreciated by your clients. For simple tasks, you can do it yourself. A monthly schedule of replacing light bulbs, testing smoke alarms and fire extinguishers, replacing or cleaning furnace filters, seasonal cleanup and other basic home maintenance can be established, and can be a popular offering for seniors or other clients with reduced mobility.

> TIP: Outdoor pools require six to eight hours a week of regular maintenance, and in most climates a day of opening in the spring and closing in the fall. If you live in an area where pools are common, consider adding this maintenance item to your service list.

When your client has some time, do a walkthrough of their home or ask them to prepare a list of projects they have been putting off. Use a home inspection list, covering the basics like roof, electrical, plumbing, outdoors, etc. Add any renovation or decorating ideas to the list as well.

You then turn this list into a schedule, and start getting these things done for your client.

Keep a log book of what repairs and maintenance were done when, as well as photocopies of the invoices. Use a system to remind you when upcoming maintenance is due. For bigger projects such as landscaping, spring cleaning or renovations you can offer to find and interview contractors, solicit quotes for your clients to look through, and arrange access to the home while the contractors work.

The latter service can also be useful when the client is installing new services such as satellite, phone, or cable, where the service people can't give a time but tell you what day they will be coming. You can save your client the hassle of sitting around waiting. When contractors do a particularly good job, add them to your list of contacts for future projects.

Angie's List is a useful tool to locate reputable contractors in your area. Membership (a.k.a. access to the list) is currently $17 for the first year. Visit the Angie's List website at **www.angieslist.com/AngiesList**.

Personal Items

You can ask your clients if they have household items, clothing or sports equipment in need of repair. Inquire about shoes, watches, clothes that need alternations, loose buttons, broken jewelry, skates, skis and snowboards that are dull, or clocks that have stopped working. You can create a checklist of frequent needs that you add to over time.

2.1.4   Pets and Families

Pets, children and extended family create many service opportunities for the business-minded personal concierge. The so-called "sandwich generation" looks after not only the needs of their children but also cares for their aging parents, and frequently find themselves stretched thin on time. You can help by taking over some time-consuming tasks for them.

Children

Personal concierges are often asked to plan birthday parties for children, arrange or drive them to appointments, and to research childcare options. You can also look into local or private schools for families who are new to an area, interview tutors, and compare summer camps for parents.

If you plan to include babysitting on your list of services, make your insurance provider aware. There may be a premium you'll pay on your policy, but you'll want to ensure you are covered in case of emergency. You'll also want to add CPR and first-aid training to your skill set. If you don't want to mind children, set this exclusion out in an initial consultation with clients (or in your letter of agreement) so you are clear.

"One of my clients asked me a few times to look after her children while she went for a jog. Not that they were ever any trouble, but I always felt a bit uncomfortable with the situation. It also distracted me from the task at hand, which was organizing paperwork in her office," recalls former personal concierge Jennifer James.

Extended Family

Extended family may create opportunities for you to send birthday or other gifts, and pack and mail care packages. With seniors, caregivers can ask you to stop in to see if there is anything they need. Something like turning off a "child lock" function on the microwave can be a quick fix for you, but a major source of frustration for a 90-year-old. Ensure senior clients are aware that you are not a medical service provider, though.

> TIP: Add the family's birthdays and notable events into your own organizer or client database, and call to remind your clients of events in advance to see what business opportunities you can create.

Pet Care

Pets are an important part of people's families too, and are not to be overlooked. You can drive crated pets to and from vet appointments, groomers, and doggy spas. When owners are away, pets need to be fed, played with, and walked; litter scooped; and health monitored.

When pet sitting you should have emergency numbers for the vet and a 24-hour animal emergency service on hand, and ask clients to sign a release for emergency treatment. To add to your credibility, consider becoming a member of the following organizations:

- *The National Association of Professional Pet Sitters (NAPPS)*
  www.petsitters.org

- *Pet Sitters International (PSI)*
  www.petsit.com

- *All Canadian Pet Services Network*
  www.acpsn.com

Not a pet person? You're not alone! "I do not provide pet sitting because I believe you should really be an individual who enjoys pets — however, I have no problem referring a good pet sitting company for clients who desire that," explains Delmar Johnson of The Concierge Place.

2.1.5   Other Personal Services

Anything that is time-consuming, tedious or the kind of thing people put off can be added to your list of personal or domestic services. Although the services you undertake are limited only to your imagination, it's best to try to anticipate what your most frequent requests may be.

Online Research

Not everyone is skilled at using Google or other search engines, and many people fail to recognize the wide range of resources available on the Internet. If you are a skilled online researcher and are tuned in to what is out there, you can help your clients immensely. For example, you might:

- Research statistics or market trends for entrepreneurs

- Compare amenities at travel resorts

- Use Epinions or Consumer Reports Online to compare products for the client

- Recommend new books based on past preferences

- Search eBay or Craigslist for items your client collects

- Find vendors for unique gifts

- Show your client the latest online hotspots

- Bookmark sites related to your clients' interests or hobbies

"One of my clients had me research and write content for a newsletter for her husband's business. She determined the topics and made out a few notes, and directed me to research materials. I then wrote and laid out a monthly newsletter for them, which they used to promote her complementary service,"

— Jennifer James, former personal concierge

Holiday Preparations

In the planning stages of starting your personal concierge business, you should sit down with a calendar and make a list of seasonal changes or events that might create opportunities for you, such as holidays, local events, etc.

Holidays are the time to:

- Buy and put up decorations

- Install lights

- Update mailing lists and generate labels

- Bake homemade treats

- Purchase and mail cards or greetings

- Plan parties

- Greet trick-or-treaters and hand out candy

- Arrange romantic dinners

- Update seasonal wardrobes

- Pack for the cottage, cruise, or the ski hill

Transportation Service

Some personal concierges include transportation service for their clients, their families, and their business colleagues. However, many don't.

"I currently exclude transport of people, in large part due to liability and the potentially high cost of commercial insurance that's required," says Delmar Johnson of The Concierge Place in Raleigh, NC.

You can compensate for the extra expenses by charging a premium for transportation service, to account for mileage, gas, insurance and wear and tear. Ask your lawyer if your clients should sign a waiver to help protect you against liability. Also, depending where you live you may require a chauffeur's license or other similar certification to legally transport people. So be sure to check into your state's licensing requirements before you offer this service.

Transportation service request might include pick-up and drop off of children at school or team practice, airport drop off and pick up, downtown drop off or pick up, pick up from eye appointments, or day travel to a nearby big city. If you want to offer this service, you'll need reliable, comfortable transportation — a minivan, while not so "cool," can be a good option for family or group transport.

If you don't want to offer transportation services, make sure you are well connected with service providers in your area. You can arrange partnerships with a preferred limo service, taxi company, or airport shuttle. One option is a flat rate or discount for your clients, based on being a preferred service provider. However, the best choice is always the company who is safe, fast, and reliable.

Even More Services to Add

Listen to your clients carefully to find out if any of the following tasks or services is needed. The more you take off their hands, the more you make yourself an indispensable part of their lives.

- Booking appointments

- Reminder service

- Assembling Ikea-style furniture

- Framing and hanging artwork

- Selling used items in newspaper classifieds, eBay, or Craigslist

- Getting prints of digital photos, making DVD slideshows, arranging albums

- Filling out paperwork

- Finding qualified contractors or service providers

- Installing new software on the computer

- Applying for name changes or passports

2.2 Shopping Services

Shopping can be a lot of fun. However, when there's no time in the day, shopping becomes a burden and an annoyance. Getting paid to shop with someone else's money might seem like a dream come true to you. If so, you'll be happy to learn that shopping for gifts, groceries and personal items will be a large part of the services you provide.

2.2.1 Groceries

Grocery shopping is a task many busy people are eager to delegate. To plan a grocery schedule for your clients, you'll need to know how many people typically eat there, and for which meals; the frequency the client wants fresh food in the house (daily, weekly, semi-monthly); and their shopping budget. You should fill out a client information form that lists the following:

- Food allergies

- Brand preferences (create a checklist)

- Preferred vendors

- Special diets (organic, vegan, South Beach)

- A "do not buy" list

- Favorite dishes

You can get some information by doing an inventory of the pantry before each shop. Alternately, you can prepare a menu for the week for your clients using some of their favorite recipes or your own. The client can approve the menu, and then checks the pantry and indicates by checking the box what foods are needed for you to pick up. Clients appreciate not having to come up with last-minute dinner ideas, and the peace of mind knowing all ingredients are on hand.

Ask your clients to let you know well in advance if they are planning to entertain guests, or if they have a special meal or food item in mind. You can incorporate these plans into your weekly menu. If a client wants unique items like chocolate or imported cheeses, you may need to visit high-end vendors or specialty shops. Your extra time and mileage are added to the bill.

> **TIP:** Have Costco and Sam's Club memberships in place *before* you take on clients, and remember that the cost will be tax-deductible.

Some clients may prefer that you "prep" ingredients by washing, chopping and storing them. Limited personal cheffing could prove to be a profitable sideline for your business. While no health licensing is necessary provided you prepare food in the client's home, be sure to follow safe food handling procedures.

If clients will be home when you deliver the groceries, you can give them the receipt and be paid on the spot. If clients won't be home, you will have to invoice them at a later date, or ask them to prepay a certain amount to you that can be debited over time. Usually the solution that makes things easiest for the client (while still ensuring you get paid promptly) is the best option.

2.2.2   Personal Shopping

While some of your clients will hire their own dedicated personal shoppers, others may want you to step in on occasion and take over this role for them. The key to successful personal shopping is to get to know clients and their preferences as much as possible in advance, so that what you select for them can be an expression of their own tastes.

While shopping trips can be simple, some may require some resourcefulness on your part. Be prepared to check out a variety of vendors, including online sources. After the 2007 Academy Awards, the Washington Post reported that a personal concierge service was successful in tracking down for their clients three $6,000 replicas of the gown actress Jennifer Lopez had worn to the event!

In some cases, the client will have a specific purchase in mind: for example a new washer/dryer set, a laptop, or office furniture. You will ask about the features they are looking for in the item, any brand or vendor preferences, and an approximate budget. You'll also want to find out how frequently the item will be used, where it will be placed, and who will use it.

Once you have gathered the relevant information, you can compare brands, vendors, and prices. For less expensive items, you can make the purchase for the client and be reimbursed on delivery. For big-ticket items you may want to make a few recommendations, and then let the client choose and arrange payment. You can still handle delivery or pick up of the items, but in the meantime you aren't out of pocket for the expense.

In general, you should look for good-quality items for your clients that will last. Check consumer reports and customer reviews, and always find out about the return policy in case the client dislikes the item or changes his or her mind. To save time, you can phone vendors ahead of time to confirm availability, and/or have them set the item aside for pick-up.

If you will be doing a lot of shopping for a client, they may authorize you in writing to use their credit card. Alternately, some vendors will allow you to take things home for your client "on approval" so they can decide if it works for them. You can also offer the service of returning items the client purchased but was dissatisfied with.

Some clients will give you very little direction about what they want, and the choices will be up to you. For example, you may end up shopping for new clothing for a mid-winter cruise, or to pack for an upcoming business trip. You will want to complete (or have the client complete) a questionnaire that helps you determine taste-based preferences as well as sizes.

> **TIP:** If your target market includes seniors, expect occasionally that your elderly clients want you to accompany them on a personal shopping trip. You can help people with reduced mobility carry bags, reach items, and get around the stores.

2.2.3   Gifts

Your typical client will have many occasions in both their personal life and business happenings when giving a gift is appropriate. Holidays, anniversaries, birthdays, grand openings, graduations, coming-of-age celebrations, and the birth of a child are all occasions to give, and your client may also want to send a gift as a token of appreciation or thanks.

It's easy to get stumped on what to buy someone as a gift — or sometimes, to even remember what you bought them last year. People panic and end up giving gifts that are just garbage or clutter. Personal concierges can add value to their service by having a great supply of sources on hand for unique gifts that will be appreciated.

Gift Ideas

You can get great gift ideas from newspapers, flyers, catalogs, and by asking friends and colleagues. Keep up with trends online and through other media, and keep notes on current sales and prices, especially as the holidays approach. As we'll explain in more detail later in this guide, good relationships with florists, chocolate vendors, or wine merchants might get you what you need after-hours.

One idea is to maintain a "tickler" file with ideas for future gifts. Alternately, you can keep an actual gift inventory of small, generic items or store gift cards to use in a pinch. Have a variety of gift wrap, cards and stamps on hand at all times. Making your own gift baskets can also be a smart way to add to your bottom line.

Holiday Shopping

For the holidays, start your gift search well in advance. In an article written for the Montreal Gazette, personal concierge Paula Quinn explained that their approach to the holidays began in October and November, when they went through the stores and made lists of what was hot for Christmas. She says that they "scouted toys, sporting goods, novelties, clothing for teens, music stores, and electronic equipment," and then gave the list to their clients.

Around the holidays you can also suggest a small number of "gift packages" that include a couple of items that work well together — for example, a "Pamper Mom" gift package for Mother's Day, which includes a luxurious bathrobe, slippers, and a gift certificate for a manicure or pedicure. The easier you can make gift selection for your clients, the more appreciated you will be.

Keeping Track of Gifts

You can add value to your service for regular clients if you keep a schedule for them of gifts to be sent. You can also ask the client for feedback on how the gift was received, and record recipients' preferences with a questionnaire such as the one on the next page, reproduced from the *FabJob Guide to Become a Personal Shopper*.

Gift Questionnaire

- What is the occasion?

- Who are the gifts for (e.g. family, friends, employees)?

- How many gifts will be needed in total?

- What date are the gifts needed for?

- Do you have any gifts in mind?

- What is your total budget?

- What is your budget per gift?

- Do you want the items to be gift-wrapped?

- Do you want a message included on a card with the gifts?

- Where do you want the gifts delivered?

- Should everyone get the same gift or will different gifts be needed for different categories of people (e.g. major clients, new clients, other clients)?

- What types of gifts have you given in the past?

- Did you receive any feedback about those gifts?

- Would you like your logo or company slogan to be included on the gift?

- What do you hope to achieve with these gifts (e.g. thank you, remember an occasion)?

- Is there anything that should not be purchased for any reason?

- After I bring you some gift recommendations, how long will the decision-making process take?

You can also keep a registry of gifts received. This helps your clients make sure a thank-you card is sent, and may spark ideas for future gift-giving as well.

Additional Gift Information

Additional information about the recipient can assist in coming up with good gift choices, especially if the gift-giver does not have gift preferences. Please provide some details below.

General

Male or Female: _____
Age (or age range): _____
Profession: _____

Hobbies or Interests *(check all that apply)*:

❑ Travel   ❑ Music   ❑ Gardening

❑ Games   ❑ Home   ❑ Workaholic

❑ Outdoor Activities   ❑ Sports (both participating and spectator)

❑ Entertaining   ❑ The arts (art, theatre, opera, ballet)

❑ Food and drink   ❑ Pampering (e.g. spa visits)

❑ Reading   ❑ Other:

Sizes *(if clothing may be purchased)*:

Dress Size: _____
Jacket Size (Men): _____
Shirt Size (Men): _____ neck   _____ arm
Pant Size: _____ inseam   _____ waist
Other: _____

Likes and Dislikes *(brands, colors, styles, previous gifts, etc.)*:

Likes

_____
_____

Dislikes

_____
_____

2.3   Travel and Entertainment Arrangements

Making travel and entertainment arrangements for your clients requires a certain amount of savvy, but is not terribly different from doing it for yourself. Here are guidelines for this service request.

2.3.1   Travel Planning and Booking

The Internet has drastically changed the way that business and personal travel is planned and booked. The challenge for most people is the overwhelming amount of information and purchasing options it provides, and the time it takes to find what you want. If you have experience researching travel products and booking them, you can offer these services.

Today there are fewer brick-and-mortar travel agencies, and fewer/smaller commissions for agents. Any service that doesn't earn a commission, such as planning itineraries or booking airline tickets, comes at a service fee to the traveler. Also, the reality today is that there are often lower prices available on the Internet for consumers than travel consultants have access to.

Tell your personal concierge clients that by planning and booking their travel, you may actually be able to save them money by:

- Avoiding service fees from travel consultants
- Comparing travel products to find the best price
- Freeing up clients' time for income-generating activities

Travel Planning

Your clients will likely have a basic idea of the travel experience they are looking for: for example, beach, mountains, resort, cruise, etc. Get some details from them before you start your research, to help you refine the choices you present them. Do they want to do sightseeing? What is the approximate budget they have in mind? Will they bring the children, or make arrangements for them? Are they looking to relax, or to keep busy? What amenities are desired?

Some clients may want you to go all out and plan a daily itinerary for them. You'll need to advise them of times they need to catch transportation, and where they need to be at what time, right down to minor details. Information on health advisories, local attractions, and even what to pack can be part of your full-service travel planning.

Listening to your client and qualifying their needs is important. You want to know a) what they like, b) where they've been, and c) what they're looking for in a vacation. If you've listened well, you may even be able to suggest a different or better option than what the client had in mind, so long as it still meets his or her needs.

When you feel like you have a grasp on what they are looking for, it's time to turn to the Internet. Online travel resources abound, and are too numerous to list in this guide. If you are overwhelmed, you can also call a travel consultant and give him or her the details. Most agents are willing to do some basic research for clients in order to land a sale.

Once you have them, present some options to your clients. It's best to have some print-outs for them to review if you meet in person, or simply email the information and links they need to follow. "Suggest two, maybe three suppliers that fit, not ten," advise the authors of the *FabJob Guide to Become a Travel Consultant*. "Too many choices cause confusion."

Booking Travel

In addition to planning travel, your clients may also prefer that you make reservations for them at hotels, with rental car agencies, and for air travel. You'll have the choice of booking online, or using a trusted travel consultant to assist you. Over time you'll discover what works best for you and your clients.

Your attention to detail will be very important when booking travel, and it all goes back to knowing the right questions to ask: does your client prefer a window or an aisle seat? Bulkhead for extra leg room in economy, or are they first-class all the way? Hotel room that faces the river or the city? Does he or she need Internet connection in the room?

It would be a good idea to put together a travel preferences questionnaire for your regular clients, and keep these on file. Add to the notes every time you book travel for your client, so you can perfect the way you offer service. The following sample questionnaire is from the *FabJob Guide to Become a Travel Consultant*.

Travel Preferences Questionnaire

The form should start with the basic info you'll need on each client, such as name of each traveler, date of birth, and citizenship. Questions for this form may include some or all of the following, depending on the services you offer and your chosen specialty. Below are some qualifying questions to help get you started.

- What kind of travel experience do you want? For example, domestic or foreign travel? A city or the countryside? The mountains or the beach?

- What is the purpose of your travel? For example, will you pursue a hobby?

- Do you wish to visit historical or educational areas, such as a War Memorial or air/space museum?

- Is this a family gathering? Will there need to be activities for the children?

- Do you want lots of action, or do you prefer quiet relaxation?

- When do you want to travel? Summertime when the weather is warm, or fall to see the colors changing? Remind clients that prices change for a destination between its high season, "shoulder" season and low season; and that depending on the destination, seasons may be reversed. For example, our winter is South America's summer.

- What type of package do you want? Perhaps an all-inclusive package with air, accommodations, meals and gratuities?

- Are you interested in a fully escorted tour, or the freedom of independent travel?

- How much do you want to spend? Would you rather spend more money on entertainment, and less on the accommodations?

- Families traveling with children or pets may want to know if a resort has children's programs, babysitting services, or if they allow cats or dogs to stay.

- Elderly travelers may have dietary or medical requirements to make the travel supplier aware of. Travelers may need wheelchair assistance on the airplane and onto the cruise ship; or a certain tour may be at a pace too strenuous for them.

Once you have gathered this initial information, you'll want to get the go-ahead to start researching travel options for the client, especially if you will be developing an itinerary.

"Some consultants will charge an upfront fee (sometimes called a "plan-to-go" fee) in order to make sure that if the client changes their mind about booking the travel, the consultant's time is still compensated. You may be hesitant to charge such a fee, but if a client is serious about booking travel they shouldn't have a problem putting a percentage of their estimated travel budget down. If a client balks at this request, this is a red flag that they are just shopping around for ideas, and are not serious about booking a trip in the near future. Some clients may just not be worth the trouble."

— *The FabJob Guide to Become a Travel Consultant*

If you expect you will book a large amount of travel, you may want to look into partnering with a local travel agency or a host agency which you can find online. You can find information about working with a host agency from the website of The National Association of Commissioned Travel Agents (NACTA), along with links to host agencies at **www.nacta.com/host_list.aspx?type=alpha**.

Most agencies will offer their affiliates a commission on travel products booked through them, based on how much business you generate. A 50/50 split of commissions is typical, but not standard.

2.3.2   Dining, Events, and Entertainment

The traditional role of a hotel concierge — reservations and tickets — is still a requested service. Your clients will ask you to book tickets for upcoming events, make reservations at local restaurants, and reserve tee times for their group. Get a list of your client's preferences, and make the call. Most reservations don't require a deposit.

While many requests like movie tickets will be straightforward, sometimes you will be asked to perform "the impossible," meaning sold-out events, private tours or dining, etc. Building relationships with key personnel at venues, restaurants, etc. will help you get what you need when you need it. You can stop by and introduce yourself, and/or send a note and a small treat to help your name be remembered fondly. If you wait until you need something to make contact, you won't have as much success.

> **TIP:** If you send enough clients their way, you may be able to negotiate preferred rates with local restaurants for your business. Always ask clients to mention if you have referred them.

It will make your life easier if you can anticipate clients' needs and respond early. An article in the *Montreal Gazette* reports that when major entertainment shows are announced, local personal concierges Karen and Paula Quinn email their clients and ask them if they will be requiring tickets. This of course saves the inevitable panic once the show is already sold out.

If you are in the position of looking for hard-to-find tickets, you can check the local newspaper, eBay, or online ticket brokers or intermediaries like the ones listed below (there are many more online). These services also have free membership options that include advance notification for events and shows coming to your area. Using this service, you can immediately let clients know when a favorite event (music, sports, theatre, etc.) is coming and purchase tickets for them.

- *Tickets Now*
  www.ticketsnow.com

- *Stub Hub*
  www.stubhub.com

- *Ticketmaster*
  www.ticketmaster.com

Be sure to ask your regular clients or preferred service providers what season tickets they have, too, and keep track. If there is a client looking for hard-to-find tickets, and another with those same tickets they won't be using, you can offer both clients the service of buying/selling tickets. In a pinch you can also call other personal concierges you know to see if they have any connections.

2.3.3 House Sitting

Clients who travel frequently will be happy to hear you provide house-sitting services. Often combined with pet sitting (as explained in section 2.1.4), house sitting generally entails stopping by once or twice a day to pick up the mail, watering plants or gardens, and making sure that all is well. Keeping in touch with clients from time to time with a quick email and letting them know things are fine at home will be appreciated.

If pets are home alone you may feed, walk and entertain them for a short while. Some parents have better peace of mind knowing someone is checking daily on teens who are home alone, or stocking the fridge for them while they are gone. Upon the client's return, you may be asked to shop and fill the fridge for them as well.

If clients will be away for a long period of time, they may want you to locate someone to stay and live on-premises. This can be a service, or it can be set up in a rental or sub-lease arrangement. For example, if a client has a vacation home that they only use for one month a year, they may want to let it out in the meantime to a family who will maintain the grounds and so on.

It's important to keep client privacy and security in mind when you house sit. Keys or security codes that have been left for you should be stored safely, and never identified with addresses or other personal information. Consider using a coded/encrypted system to store and locate keys and access codes, which is not obvious to anyone but you.

If you would like to get some experience in this area, you can find a short-term or longer-term job through the Internet. There are a number of websites, such as **www.mindmyhouse.com**, that connect house sitters with people needing this service. Some of these jobs are in exotic locations, but there are lots of jobs available in the U.S. as well. Job terms range from a week or two to more than a year. Type "house sitter" or "house sitting" into a search engine like Google to find more opportunities. You can also place an ad offering your services as a house sitter.

You should always use caution and common sense when applying for positions like these, or advertising your services as a house sitter. Insist on having an initial meeting in a public place, for example. Take a cell phone or a friend with you if possible. Be sure to let family or friends know what you're doing. Ask for references.

2.4   Party/Special Occasion Planning

There's nothing better than throwing a fabulous party where people are laughing and having a good time. But planning a party is a lot of work, and there are so many details involved that your busy clients will want your help so their event can be perfect from start to finish.

For big events you might prefer to refer clients (or subcontract) to a trusted event planner who can do it up right. For smaller get-togethers, or even romantic dinners for two, the personal concierge can assist with planning food and drink, setting a mood, and decorating.

If the thought of planning a party leaves you feeling decidedly un-festive, you can learn all you need to know (and add dollars to your bottom line) with some quick study. The information in the following section is adapted from the *FabJob Guide to Become a Party Planner* by Jackie Larson and Craig Coolahan, a complete resource to offering this service.

2.4.1   Invitations and Theme

Like most tasks you take on for your client, you'll start with a meeting to get the details straight. The client may have a budget in mind, or they may give you some parameters and ask you to put together a proposal. Ask the client to tell you about the theme or purpose of the event, a few potential dates/times for the event they have in mind, approximate number of guests, and any ideas they have for food or decorating.

A theme is a unifying concept that flows through the party. It links the food and drink, the invitations, the décor and all the creative parts of the party together. A theme should have a cohesiveness that reflects the personality of the host, as well as the objective of the party.

A theme can be based on a seasonal change, a popular movie, a specific food, or even a particular color. The client may have specific creative elements they want to include in the party, which you can jot down to work with. You'll also add your own creativity into the mix.

Your client should have a guest list prepared, or at least an idea of how many people are likely to be invited or attend. Let your client know if you can design and print invitations, prepare mailing labels, or receive RSVPs. You can either sit down with your client and take notes, or ask them to email you a list of invitees and contact information.

If you plan to print labels, the guest list needs to be typed and formatted to fit neatly on a mailing label. You can print the labels yourself on a home computer, or have a printer generate and/or affix them for you. For last-minute parties, email or phone invitations might be a necessity.

> **TIP:** Keep a record in your client folders or database of any events you plan, so you have a basis of understanding for the next one. The more you know your clients, the more personalized (and valuable) service you can offer.

2.4.2 Food and Drink

While your client may be a do-it-yourself kind of person, let him or her know that leaving the food and drink to the experts is often a wise decision. Instead of spending all day and night defrosting, prepping, popping things in and out of the oven, and serving, a catering company can handle these details for your clients, leaving them free to entertain and enjoy their guests.

Get an approximate per-person budget from your client for food and drink, and ask them if they have worked with a particular caterer in the past that they have liked. If not, you can meet with your preferred caterer or personal chef for ideas, or if you are looking for more selection you can call up a few and compare menus.

Your client will decide whether they want to serve a sit-down multi-course dinner, a buffet-style spread, or simply stick with snacks and drinks. Find out if your client will require servers, which adds to the bill somewhat. Alternately, your clients may prefer to make food on their own, or make some of the meal and order the rest. Suggest that they make whatever they have in mind in advance and freeze it, though, since there are many other things to tend to the day of the party.

The key to a successful food selection is variety and simplicity. Even things that seem a sure bet, such as a cheese platter, are not foolproof. Work in as much variety to the menu as possible by serving smaller amounts of a greater selection of items.

2.4.3   Music/Entertainment

Music selections can range from background strings and harp music, to a live band that's the center of attention. While low background music is nice for the cocktail hour, you will want to pump up the volume if the guests want to dance. The kind of music you arrange will depend on the demographics of the party guests. You and the host might consider any or a mix of the following:

- A live band

- An orchestral trio

- A DJ spinning tunes

- A soloist

- A pre-recorded mix CD

- A selection of favorite albums

Many different entertainment options are available for parties. Clowns, magicians, and novelty acts often specialize in kids' parties, although some gear their act towards adults. Entertainment can add real pizzazz to a party, especially if it fits in with the overall theme. Some fun options include:

- Caricaturists

- Casino dealers

- Comedians

- Dancers

- Fortune tellers or psychics

- Hypnotists

- Impressionists or look-alikes

- Massage therapists

- Lounge-style piano player

You can put together a contact sheet for each entertainment act that includes their contact info, rates, availability, and if they supply all their own equipment, and attach it to their press kit. Keep these on file for the future, and update them periodically.

2.4.4   Decorating

Decorating for the party can be simple, or transport guests to another world, depending on the look you are going for. Decorating for your own child's party might be limited to a printed paper tablecloth and colored streamers, but as a personal concierge it's up to you to take things up a notch.

Consider how color, mood and theme factor into the selection of décor elements such as:

- Centerpieces
- Lighting
- Linens
- Flowers
- Serving trays
- Furniture arrangement
- Place cards

Flowers are always a popular decorative touch, since they add both beauty and scent. You may decide to hire a florist to handle flower selection and delivery, but it is advised that you have some ideas of what your client is looking for before setting a meeting. Know whether they want their flowers to be understated or bold.

Different lighting from what we are used to every day creates mood and ambiance. Because they serve the double-role of decoration and alternative light source, candles are a popular choice for party lighting. From tea lights to scented candles to pillars, candles can transform any space. Tiki torches, paper lanterns and colored bulbs are fun choices as well for themed events.

Meeting or Company Party Planning

If you work with entrepreneurs or executives as your clients, your assistance may be requested to plan meetings and/or company parties. The biggest difference is that the event will be held offsite, so your selection of an appropriate venue is critical.

For example, meeting planners need to consider the facilities of conference rooms, local available hotels and transportation, audiovisual equipment needs, and amenities of the meeting space. When booking company parties, you'll be looking for a place that is unique (i.e., not the same place as last year), as private as needed, and of course, not already sold out.

Having relationships established in advance is a help. Check out the conference facilities of local hotels, and fill out check sheets to compare amenities. Meet face-to-face with key personnel, and get contact names on file. In the fall you can do a round-up of the available spaces for holiday parties, and let your clients choose. You'll then follow up and make the booking.

2.5 Executive Assistance

Personal concierges can be asked to provide office help to those without a full-time executive assistant, but who have an occasional need for one. Busy entrepreneurs, executives, and business people who travel a lot may need executive assistance from time to time. You may be hired by the individuals, or sometimes hired by the company that employs them.

Many executive assistant-type tasks can be completed with little or no contact with the individual needing help. Sending faxes, typing out handwritten notes, or drafting press releases can all be done unsupervised, and often from your home. This kind of service is sometimes called a virtual assistant, and a concept that is growing in popularity.

Concierges who focus entirely on corporate business often refer to themselves as "corporate concierges." If you choose to make this your specialty, you may want to increase your training in this direction —

making sure you can type quickly, know how to send a UPS package, and are well-versed in PowerPoint, for example.

2.5.1 Technology Solutions

Business people have little time to figure out the technology that makes them more efficient — they just need it to work. You can develop a profitable niche troubleshooting technology glitches for your clients, or simply helping them get electronically organized.

If you have the skills, consider adding the following services to your techno-menu:

- Software and update installation

- Virus and adware scans

- Error message troubleshooting

- Transferring a physical address book or day planner to an electronic one

- Organizing and storing photos and music

- Quick introduction to/troubleshooting popular software programs

- Demonstrating how to sync technologies

- Updating (or demonstrating how to update) websites

- Organizing a cluttered email inbox

- Setting up a file system for clients' computers

- Analyzing and improving e-security

To keep up with the latest trends you can read technology magazines or websites, or at a minimum read the "technology" section of the newspaper.

2.5.2 Office Help

When it comes to office help, any way you can add time to your clients' schedules or put money back into their pockets will be appreciated, from filing, to organizing, making copies or sending faxes, arranging for parcel pick-up, and taking inventory.

According to Tag and Catherine Goulet, authors of the book *Dream Careers*, you need to demonstrate that you bring those who hire you more value than your cost. "Value is perceived a bit differently by each employer, depending on where they need assistance, but two constants are time and money," they explain. Two examples they offer:

- Freeing up your client's time so she can do more important work and/or make more money (taking over some of her tasks, or helping her get better organized)

- Reducing your client's frustration by doing tasks he doesn't like doing himself (common examples include filing, making coffee, responding to emails, communicating with lower-level employees, typing, etc.)

Again, the key to success is to find out where help is needed. Ask your clients what sources of frustration they are currently experiencing, or what important work they would do if they could have some time free of administrative tasks. Use their answers to suggest ways you can help.

Writing and Proofreading

Your entrepreneur clients may be very talented at running their businesses, but that doesn't mean that they are skilled at communication. Many very intelligent people struggle with writing press releases, blog entries, fact sheets, newsletters, or even business correspondence and emails. They can't find the right words, and then they worry that they've made themselves look silly with a bunch of grammatical errors.

> **TIP:** Offering writing and proofreading services to your clients can be a valuable sideline, and is a great one-time service to get yourself established as a "helper" in their lives.

"I landed two of my clients through an initial contact about my writing and proofreading services. It turned out that these people had many pots simmering at the same time, but not enough to justify full-time help. When they asked me to take on some personal concierge work as well, I was happy to add to my billable hours," says guide author Jennifer James.

2.6   Relocation Service

Coordinating any move is a lot of work, and you don't get time off your job to do it. Especially when people are being transferred for work, they'll be busy enough organizing the job transfer without having to worry about updating their address with the magazines they subscribe to. There are a lot of ways a personal concierge can help people coming and going, as detailed in this section. If you want to make relocation a specialty for your concierge service, make sure to build your referral network with the people who can help you the most, such as:

- Moving companies

- Packing services

- Real estate lawyers

- Realtors

- Mortgage specialists

- Home stagers

- Landscape companies

While some of their services will compete with yours, there will always be something they don't want to do. Meeting with people new to the area will also help you introduce your services early, at a time when they are most needed. With the right approach, your relocation clients may turn into future "regulars."

2.6.1   Evaluating Homes and Rentals

If your clients are moving to the town or city from far away, they can benefit greatly from having a go-to person on site. You can first help them find and hire a reputable real estate agent. If the client sees a listing for a property they are interested in, you can arrange to visit and see how it compares to what they need. You can offer clients an objective perspective on homes or condos they are considering.

If they are unfamiliar with the city or region, clients will appreciate an insider's opinion of what neighborhoods suit them best. You can also check crime rates, evaluate the nearby schools, and even spend a few hours finding out how often the prospective neighbors come and go. Contact the city and community association, and provide your clients with a list of:

- Local schools and their reputations

- Nearby parks and amenities

- Closest shopping

- Transportation and carpooling options

- Local bylaws or easements

- Planned improvements to roads or sewers

When an offer is made and accepted, you can assist clients by running paperwork where it needs to go, calling and setting up appointments with inspectors, doing walkthroughs, and being the eyes and ears of your clients whenever they need them. You can arrange to ship inspection reports out to your client ASAP for their consideration.

On the home front, you can also assist clients who are selling by acting as on-site security during open houses, or hiring and coordinating contractors to make improvements. You may also be asked to hire a home stager, or add to your services and make staging improvements yourself to help the client's home sell quickly and for more money. (These helpful services are especially valuable to the client who has already moved to their new location.)

2.6.2   Moving and Storage Arrangements

As a personal concierge, you can help your clients navigate the moving process with ease. Take the unwanted task of packing off their hands by doing it yourself, or hiring professionals. You can call moving companies and get quotes from them for your clients, which can be a time-consuming process.

You can arrange to sell unneeded items for your clients, through a classified directory (you take the calls) or a garage sale if the client agrees. If overflow items will need to be stored locally or at the new location, you can source some reputable storage companies and make the arrangements.

Clients planning a cross-country move will need to arrange travel for themselves and family, including booking hotels and/or flights. You can help your clients keep organized by preparing an itinerary of days leading up to the move, any time in-limbo, and the days after they move in. Include key details such as which installers are coming when, what day to read the hydro meter, the times of their flights, and the address of the hotel they are staying at.

Clients may also require document and progress management with a local lawyer; hiring contractors for repairs, improvements, and cleaning; and purchasing appliances and arranging for their delivery. You can also get quotes for new home or condo insurance for them, and call the local utilities to make sure everything will be running on move-in day.

2.6.3 Settling-In Services

Especially if clients have used your services to relocate, it's a nice touch to have a Welcome basket awaiting their arrival. The basket can include fresh fruit or home-baked cookies, as well as coupons and brochures for local businesses and services, and contact information for the community or condominium association or Chamber of Commerce.

Other settling-in services can include researching daycare or interviewing nannies, updating addresses with friends and family, and updating billing addresses with credit card companies, etc. If the client has relocated from another state, province or country, make a list of required document changes and deadlines to switch over, providing the address of offices to contact.

In any move there is an abundance of tasks the personal concierge can assist with. Unpacking is a major chore, and best left to someone with professional organizing experience — either you or a contractor you hire. Computers, TVs and speakers need to be set up and/or installed, shelves put up, etc. If you know the area well, you can offer to take the family on an acclimatization tour.

> **TIP:** People who are new to the area make great potential clients, even if they didn't use your relocation services. You can drop off a brochure in the mailbox, or send information via a community Welcome Wagon package or program.

3. Developing Your Skills

The best personal concierges are true jacks-of-all-trades, with a set of personal skills that is both varied and specific. "The concierge industry is made for someone who is 'services' oriented," says Dustyn Shroff of One Concierge. In this chapter we'll look at some of the skills you will need as well as ways to develop these skills to become a real success in this career.

3.1 Skills Assessment

❏ Yes ❏ No   Do people frequently ask for your advice on a variety of topics?

❏ Yes ❏ No   Do you enjoy finding solutions to problems?

❏ Yes ❏ No   Are you creative and resourceful?

❏ Yes ❏ No   Do you know a variety of problem-solving techniques?

❏ Yes ❏ No   Do you have a good vocabulary?

❏ Yes ❏ No   Do people consider you to be a good listener?

❑ Yes ❑ No   Do you have excellent verbal/nonverbal/written communications skills?

❑ Yes ❑ No   Are you comfortable in the world of the well-to-do?

❑ Yes ❑ No   Are you well versed in business and social etiquette?

❑ Yes ❑ No   Are you able to maintain client confidentiality at all times?

❑ Yes ❑ No   Are you "thick-skinned"?

❑ Yes ❑ No   Can you see the big picture and break it down into manageable components?

❑ Yes ❑ No   Are you well organized?

❑ Yes ❑ No   Do you have an entrepreneurial spirit?

❑ Yes ❑ No   Do you work well without supervision?

❑ Yes ❑ No   Do you have experience running a business?

❑ Yes ❑ No   Do you meet deadlines and work well under pressure?

These 17 questions offer insight into characteristics typical of individuals who enter and succeed in the world of the personal concierge. How did you do? If you answered "yes" to all of these questions, you already have qualities found in successful personal concierges. Now look at any you answered "no." Questions 1 to 4 relate to problem-solving skills, questions 5-7 relate to your people skills, questions 8-11 relate to your ability to fit in with wealthy clients and maintaining discretion and decorum, and questions 12-17 relate to business management and self-management skills.

As we said at the start of this chapter, the skills you need to succeed as a personal concierge can be learned. So let's take a look at the specific skills that can help you succeed. Later in this chapter you'll find plenty of resources to develop these skills through education and self-study.

3.2 Problem-Solving Skills

From something relatively simple like choosing just the right gift for someone on your client's gift list, to mini-crises like knowing what to do when your client calls you from Paris to tell you that her favorite hotel where you thought you had her booked has no record of the reservation, your problem-solving skills will constantly be challenged in this business. That's a good thing, because few other careers keep you on your toes in this way and make life so interesting, challenging and variable.

As a personal concierge you will often be faced with challenges, which can sometimes seem like insurmountable obstacles, created by clients or by the vendors, contractors and suppliers you use. A variety of problems great and small will need to be solved through your ability to think on your feet. Often, you will need novel approaches to quickly resolve issues and come up with the best solutions in special circumstances. Among the most important factors in this will be your creativity, problem-solving abilities, and resourcefulness.

3.2.1 Creative Thinking

Creativity

Creativity can be defined in many different ways. Generating ideas, using your imagination, producing something new and unique, are all examples of creativity. These are all essential components of solving problems for clients, too.

Most client "problems" will not be insurmountable obstacles. Instead, a problem can be thought of as any item or service your client currently lacks, and any want or need that you can fulfill for them. So by this definition, a "problem" could be something like a client not having the time to run an errand or not having the budget to hire a full-time personal assistant. Your task in solving your client's problem is to help them find creative solutions to meet their needs.

Your creativity will also be challenged by coming up with services that fit your target market (marketing will be discussed in more detail in section 3.5.2 and section 6.1). If your expertise is in the field of retail clothing you can think of ways to put that knowledge to use as a service others might be interested in hiring you for. But take it one step further, maybe you were in management at a retail clothing store, and suddenly you have opened up even more possibilities for providing services to clients. Not only can you help them fill their closets with the latest in fashionable clothing, but you can provide on-demand expertise in scheduling, merchandising, marketing, and a host of other business-related tasks you also know how to do.

Creative Problem-Solving

It would be nice if there were always only one "right" solution to every problem that you could find by knowing enough about the situation. In fact, there are often numerous possible solutions to any problem that arises. Thus, rather than trying to find the only solution to a problem, your goal will likely be to find the "best" solution in a particular situation. In other words, you'll need to practice creative problem-solving.

Think about the following "rules" of problem-solving:

1. Don't focus on a single solution

2. No problem is insurmountable

3. The problem has been solved before

4. Solve the problem, not the symptoms

5. Solve the simplest version of the problem first

There are a variety of strategies you can use to help you find a way through, or past, a problem. You might already have your own system of problem-solving, but if not, you will probably come up with one as you develop your clientele and the services you offer them. Quite often, in almost any line of work, the same types of client issues will arise again and again (see section 3.3.4). As a result, as you gain experience, you will realize that you may have dealt with a similar situation with a client in the past.

Remember that no problem is insurmountable, and there is always some solution to any given problem. You may end up using a completely different solution than you started out with, but the important thing when you take on a new problem is to remain open-minded and flexible. Come up with as many solutions as you can so that you will have a variety to choose from in case one doesn't work out.

Remember, too, that whatever problem you encounter, someone else has probably encountered a similar problem at some time and solved it already. This is where your network of family, friends, and colleagues will come in handy. Use them and ask them for help when you need it. Never tell your clients "no" if you can avoid it. Use common sense, personal connections and creative thinking whenever possible. Sometimes you can't work miracles, but you sure look – and feel – great when you can save the day. "Don't be afraid to make mistakes and don't be afraid to take on tasks that you think may be too large," says One Concierge CEO Dustyn Shroff. "There is no better feeling than receiving a phone call or an email from a client thanking you for making their event/occasion such a success.

Another helpful tip is to solve the actual problem and not just its symptoms. For example, helping clients reduce clutter in their homes means not just hiring a maid service to come in and clean up, but also involves creating a clutter management system such as that described in section 2.1. By helping clients figure out how to stay ahead of chaos and creating a system to deal with it as it arises, you help them reduce the chances of creating the same problem in the future.

As an example of the creative problem-solving process, let's return for a moment to the woman mentioned at the start of this section who is stranded without a hotel room in Paris. In this example, the simplest version of the problem would be that the hotel has simply mixed up the reservations, so you phone the hotel yourself and inquire about the booking. They tell you that your client's name does not appear in their database at all. This is no time to start assigning blame (such as to the travel agent or online service you used to book the room); your client needs a bed for the night.

Rule Number 1 is not to focus on just one solution to the problem. Now is the time to start thinking about multiple solutions. Does the hotel have any other rooms available? If not, rather than yelling and screaming at them that you absolutely have to have a room in that hotel because that is where your client wants to stay (i.e. focusing on a single solution), the best thing you can do is ask them nicely if they can recommend another hotel nearby. If they can't or won't recommend another hotel, you quickly look up a list of hotels in Paris on the Internet and start phoning until you find a suitable room for your client.

Then you call the original hotel back and request a room for the remainder of your client's stay in Paris. She misses one night in her favorite hotel, but you do get a room for her there for the balance of her visit. Maybe when you call her back to give her the good news, she tells you that she likes the second hotel even better.

As you can see, creative problem-solving means that you keep an open mind about how you look at possible solutions and their outcomes. The next section on "Resourcefulness" will lead you through a number of different techniques you can use to come up with new ideas, generate unique solutions, and develop backup plans. There are a number of good books you can read that will help you develop creative thinking skills. One good starting point is the book, *Lateral Thinking*, by Edward de Bono, available at Amazon.com.

3.2.2   Resourcefulness

Resourcefulness goes hand in hand with problem-solving. As a personal concierge you will often encounter situations that will challenge your abilities and demand resourcefulness. If you've seen the movie "The Devil Wears Prada," you may remember that Miranda Priestly, the boss of main character Andy Sachs, asked Andy to get her a copy of the latest "Harry Potter" book before it had even been published. Because Andy knew a photographer who knew someone who worked for the publishing house that held the manuscript, she was able to meet her boss's unreasonable demand.

This is the kind of resourcefulness you may need in real-life situations as a personal concierge. Resourcefulness is really a measure of your creative thinking process and will be extremely valuable for the day-to-day running of your business, for dealing with vendors, contractors, and suppliers, and, ultimately, as you produce unique solutions to clients' problems and requests.

As you read about the techniques outlined below, think about how you can apply them to a variety of issues. For example, you might use them in coming up with ideas for client gift lists, in solving a vendor or supplier problem such as mix-ups during a party you are planning for a client, in coming up with a name for your new business venture, and so on. There are almost infinite ways that you can apply your resourceful mind to tackle almost any problem once you know a few basic techniques.

Brainstorming

Brainstorming is an idea-generating technique you can use to come up with many different options for dealing with a particular problem. You may want to have other people, such as friends or family, or business colleagues, help you with a brainstorming session (depending on the nature of the issue you're tackling).

To brainstorm effectively, make sure that there is a continuous flow of ideas without judging them as they emerge. If others are helping you, don't discuss the ideas until all the ideas have been put forward. When you let yourself talk and blurt out ideas without thinking about them, the most amazing and creative ideas can start to come out.

After you have recorded your list of ideas, you can then discuss them and you will be surprised at how many good ideas come out as you discuss the list. You can also add on to ideas already given or combine ideas to come up with yet another unique solution.

Keep a Note Pad by Your Bed

Write down any ideas that come to you as you are drifting off to sleep or when you first awake in the morning. It is proven that the brain is considered to be more creative when it is in the "Alpha" state (just before falling asleep and immediately after waking up and also while dreaming).

Develop Backup Plans

It's always a good idea to have a "Plan B" (and sometimes a Plan C) ready in case Plan A doesn't work out. You can have backup plans ready in case of a crisis for every contingency you can think of. But remember, you can't think of everything (nobody can) so you can never be prepared for every possible development.

One way to help you get a handle on this is to ask yourself "What if?" questions at every possible opportunity. For example, you might ask yourself "What would I do if my client hated every idea on the gift list I put together for her and only told me about it a week before the holiday after I've done all the shopping for her gifts?" Try to think of as many different solutions as you can to a variety of problems. Doing this exercise will develop your ability to roll with the punches, so that when something goes wrong in real life, you will be able to quickly find a solution.

Learn by Example

If you already have some experience as a personal concierge, such as an internship or working with a mentor (see section 3.6.3 for more about these), or other experience as a personal assistant, think about what you or your mentor did in a particular situation. Can you apply those solutions to your problem? Is there some element of a given solution to a certain type of problem similar to the one you now face that you can adapt?

Network with others in your industry. By having a larger pool of experience to draw on, you will probably find someone who has dealt with the same or similar problems to those you face. Talk to other personal concierges, as well as your vendors, suppliers and others with whom you do business. You'll find more about associations you can join in section 3.8.1, and read section 6.5.1 to learn more about other ways to network.

3.3 People Skills

As a personal concierge you have to be a good communicator and know how to remain cool under pressure. Ask yourself how you handle challenges and crises in your own life. Do you fly off the handle, or do you normally take a step back and think before you react? You should be a good negotiator, and your listening skills should be above average. When people call you, they will likely be stressed out. You need to defuse, solve, and assure.

"You really should be an outgoing people-person," advises personal concierge Jill Burstein. "If you can't connect on a personal level or are uncomfortable with clients, then they will be uncomfortable with you! They have to trust you and feel good about handing over all of that personal information," she notes.

Communication skills will play an enormous role in your activities as a personal concierge. As part of your job, you will be communicating verbally and in writing, with individuals and groups. This book covers essential components of those communication skills. In this section we look at the skills that can help you effectively communicate different types of messages.

3.3.1 Communications Skills

Basics of Communication

A study of face-to-face communication conducted by Albert Mehrabian at the University of California, Los Angeles, found that the percentage of the meaning conveyed through each channel of communication was as follows:

- Verbal (the actual words used) 7%

- Vocal (tone of voice and other vocal qualities) 38%

- Visual (primarily facial expressions) 55%

While these figures do not apply in most communication situations outside the research lab, this now famous study helped make people aware of the importance of vocal and visual communication. Most people intuitively know that vocal qualities, facial expressions, and body language can communicate more than words alone. For example, imagine asking someone "How are you?" If that person replies "fine" in a curt manner, with a frown on her face, and her arms crossed, chances are that person is not really "fine."

Verbal and Vocal Communication

Although in the UCLA study only seven percent of a message's meaning was conveyed through the words alone, your choice of words is also important. This is particularly true in communication situations where there are few or no visual clues, such as written communications or telephone conversations.

In all communication situations in this business, but especially in situations where you're working with a wealthy, well-educated clientele, your vocabulary will be important. You're not communicating effectively if the person you're talking or writing to doesn't understand you or is annoyed by how you speak.

In addition to vocabulary, there are many other verbal and vocal traits that may affect the way you are perceived by clients. People may make judgments about your competence, knowledge, and trustworthiness based on your accent, pronunciation, grammar, use of fillers (such as "uh" and "um"), and vocal qualities such as volume, tone, pitch, and rate of speaking.

To give one example of how vocal qualities can affect how you are perceived, consider some common stereotypes based on speech rates. In the *FabJob Guide to Become an Image Consultant*, the image experts said:

A fast-talking person may appear to others to be shifty or untrustworthy. Some people feel that fast talkers do not really know what they are saying, and their thoughts are not well reasoned out. Those who speak more slowly may be slower, more methodical thinkers. They may think carefully about what they say. The impression, however, can be that these people lack intelligence because they are "slow."

To improve your vocal communication skills, ask people you respect for feedback on any areas that could be improved. For professional assistance consider hiring a voice coach or speech coach. You may be able to find a local coach in the Yellow Pages or through the Voice and Speech Trainers Association at **www.vasta.org**.

Non-Verbal Communication

Non-verbal communication skills are especially important when you are conducting in-person coaching sessions. As the UCLA study found, non-verbal communication can be particularly powerful in such face-to-face communication. Generally, if there is conflict between the words being spoken and the message communicated by the body, the body is more likely to be believed. Controlling your non-verbal communication so that you do not inadvertently communicate negative messages is essential.

Non-verbal communication (also known as "body language") happens through facial expressions, eye contact, posture, gestures, and other body movements. Negative body movement such as fidgeting and crossed arms, and negative facial expressions such as narrowed eyes and furrowing the brow, send off signals of uneasiness and a lack of confidence, both of which are unattractive qualities in a personal concierge.

The first step to sending positive non-verbal messages is to become conscious of your body language. Notice when you make particular gestures out of habit or as a reaction to what's happening around you. Then choose to use positive body language. For example, you can control the amount of eye contact you make when interviewing someone or conversing with a client.

In North America, the person doing the talking in a conversation typically makes eye contact 40% of the time, while the listener typically makes eye contact almost 70% of the time. Those who make more eye contact without staring are perceived as more confident and interested, while those who make less eye contact may be seen as uncomfortable, bored, or hiding something.

Being sensitive to your non-verbal communication before you are actually in a communication situation such as an interview is a habit well worth developing. If you develop this awareness, using appropriate body language will come naturally to you when the pressure is on.

It is not only your own body language that is important. Reading other people's non-verbal cues can help you in your work, too. Although body language can't tell you precisely what someone is thinking, it can give you clues so you can ask follow up questions, even as basic as "How do you feel about that?"

If you want to improve this skill, you can find some excellent advice in books such as *Reading People*, by Jo-Ellan Dimitrius and Wendy Patrick Mazzarella, and *How to Read a Person Like a Book*, by Gerald I. Nierenberg and Henry H. Calero.

Listening

Going back to the movie "The Devil Wears Prada," you may remember the way that assistant Andy Sachs got her daily orders from her boss—a long string of business and personal tasks, followed by a quiet "that's all." It was up to Andy to remember names or past preferences, and when she had little else to go on, use her best judgment.

While it's unlikely that you'll be subjected to the whims of a true "Miranda Priestly," you will certainly have similar experiences with demanding clients who have specific needs, and little time to explain things twice. Your attention to detail will make you either sink or swim in this industry. (See section 3.4.1 for more about this subject.)

Writing for the *Harvard Business Review on Effective Communication*, Ralph G. Nichols and Leonard A. Stevens assert in an article titled "Listening to People," that "the effectiveness of the spoken word hinges not so much on how people talk but mostly on how they listen." As a personal concierge, understanding the needs of your clients is crucial to successful outcomes. Therefore, effective listening skills are a must.

While listening seems like an easy skill to master, most of us experience challenges in at least one of the following areas involved in listening: paying attention, understanding, and remembering. You can improve your listening skills by focusing fully on someone when they are speaking. Here are some ways to do that:

- Don't be distracted by what is going on around you. Such factors as loud noises, the other person's misuse or mispronunciation of a word, or an uncomfortable room temperature can all affect your listening.

- Avoid interrupting the other person. Allow the other person to finish speaking before jumping in with a comment or question.

- Keep listening to the other person, even if you think you know what they will say next. If you make assumptions, you may miss the point they're making.

- Pay attention to non-verbal signals (tone of voice, facial expression, body language) which may provide additional information about a speaker's emotions.

- Consider the perspective of the person talking and the context of their comments. For example, a new employee may speak in much more positive terms about a company than other employees because they are excited about being hired for their new job.

- Ask questions if you need any points clarified.

- Paraphrase what the other person has said. This allows you to confirm that you understood what they said correctly to avoid misunderstandings later.

So train your memory, but don't rely on it. You can improve your recall by taking notes during conversation, and keep detailed client files. Even seemingly unimportant details may come back to haunt you. Review or rewrite your notes often, and keep adding to them as you service a client. If things come flying at you too fast to jot them down, use a voice recorder on the job, or develop your own version of shorthand.

If information must be recalled exactly, then the conversation should be recorded if the other person consents. Additional advice to help you improve your listening skills is available online at **www.businesslistening. com.**

3.3.2   Negotiation

Being a good negotiator can help you in many ways as a personal concierge. Negotiation can help you put together the best deal possible when taking on a new client. Negotiating well can help you save money with suppliers and vendors, allowing you to either pass on the savings to your clients, or increase your profit margin.

The optimal result of any negotiation is to come away in a win-win situation for everyone. As you become more experienced and known as a personal concierge, negotiating deals with vendors will become easier because of the steady volume of sales or work you bring to them. Until you earn that kind of reputation, though, you will need to be a little more creative in your negotiating.

Here are some tips for effective negotiating:

Negotiate with the Right Person

Do not waste your time negotiating with people who do not have the authority to give you a discount. You may get along quite well with a salesperson but if their manager is the only person with the authority to make deals, then go directly to the manager.

Be Prepared

A vital part of negotiating is knowledge. If you enter into a negotiation about the price of a service without first finding out the industry average you will not know if the price the vendor is suggesting is fair or not. Do your homework and gather information on prices and other variables from as many vendors and suppliers as possible.

Come Ready to Deal

When entering a negotiation phase with a vendor, be prepared to offer something in return. If the vendor is relatively new to the marketplace and trying to build a client base, you could offer to pass out their business cards at your next networking opportunity. Come up with a list of ways your service is unique and can benefit theirs. Be ready to use that list at the negotiating table. If you are working with clients who are influential people in your city, make sure the vendor knows this.

Use Smart Negotiating Tactics

One of the best ways to ensure you are getting a good deal from a vendor or supplier is to tell them you are shopping around and getting comparative prices from their competitors. Another tactic often used is the offer of an immediate deal if the vendor or supplier reduces their price by a certain percentage. The vendor or supplier may be willing to give the discount rather than have you leave the premises to shop around.

Finally, don't be afraid to ask for what you want. The worst that can happen is that someone refuses. After all, if you are persistent and ask for three things the vendor might just give you one of them and you walk away with one more thing than you started with. Develop the ability to get people to say "yes" whether you are asking for a discount or a freebie. Always ask yourself "What's in it for them?" when approaching someone, and make sure you present those benefits.

There are many excellent resources to help you become a master negotiator. Try the book *Getting to Yes: Negotiating Agreement Without Giving In*, by Roger Fisher and William Ury, for starters. Another resource that you can find online is **www.articlealley.com/article_78409_18.html**.

3.3.3   Etiquette

The best personal concierges have an ability to move comfortably in the world of the well-to-do. You should also understand instinctively what type of information needs to be kept in confidence.

Clients will notice details about you too. Your image is important: manicures, hair style, and wardrobe must convey professionalism. Your own level of personal organization will be your saving grace, or your downfall if you let it slide because you are "too busy" with clients.

"You can't wear the same clothes you would wear on an early Saturday morning foray to the grocery store to the corporate offices, or your client's home. If you aren't going to wear something that shouts 'MY Company!' then at least dress business-casual. Neat jeans are fine. But not wrinkled track suits, dirty shoes and unkempt hair," says Jill Burstein of Jill will... Concierge Service.

Etiquette Tips

Etiquette includes having impeccable manners, of course, but this includes much more than just saying "please" and "thank you." You'll need to have knowledge of dining etiquette, business etiquette (including proper use of the telephone, email and other business communications), the proprieties of being a good conversationalist, and so on.

Dining etiquette includes a number of factors, such as how a formal place-setting is put together and what each dish and utensil is used for. You should also know different styles of eating, like American versus European. A knowledge of wines will go a long way toward making you a dining expert, as well as knowing which courses are served in what order.

Business etiquette is a subject in which clients might call upon your expertise. As mentioned in section 2.5 personal concierges are often used by busy executives who have no full-time assistant but do have an occasional need for one. In this situation, you will need to know how to properly respond to emails, the correct wording for business letters, and so on.

Another important area is telephone etiquette. Whether you are using your own business phone or fielding calls for clients be sure you know what is appropriate in a given instance. Here are some basic telephone etiquette tips:

- Let people know if you are putting them on a speaker phone, especially if someone else is in the room with you. You don't want the person on the other end to accidentally say something inappropriate in a conversation they thought was private.

- When leaving a message for others, be sure to make it easy for them to get back to you. Leave your name, your company name, a brief message outlining the purpose of your call, and leave your phone number last. Repeat your name and phone number as a courtesy (the recipient may be trying to write these down as they listen to your message).

- Make sure your voicemail or answering machine message is brief and sounds professional. Include your name, company name and request the caller's name, a message and phone number. Assure the caller you will be happy to return the call as quickly as possible.

- Observe good cell phone etiquette. For example, if you are in a meeting or other discussion with a client or anyone else you do business with, let your voicemail pick up the call rather than answering your cell phone and interrupting the conversation. Don't disrupt other people around you if you need to answer a call.

Discretion

Discretion is a most desirable quality in a personal concierge. In large part, your reputation will be built around your ability to maintain discretion with clients at all times. This is particularly true in terms of knowing what not to say about your employer or clients. Here are some tips for practicing discretion:

- Avoid passing on rumors or gossip

- Don't tell questionable stories or jokes

- Do not dwell on personal misfortunes, especially those that are current

- Don't delve into your health problems and concerns or a client's health (unless the other person is suffering from something obvious and temporary, such as wearing a cast for a broken limb)

- Avoid discussing religious and political affiliations, as these often create heated debate

- Avoid discussing controversial subjects, especially if you don't know where the other person stands. If these topics do come up, try to take a neutral stance when you are with clients, business associates, or others you don't know well, even if you hold strong opinions on the subject.

- Avoid talking about negative items in the news (for example, divorce or bankruptcy), as you don't know what the other person is experiencing or has gone through in the past.

Remember that you will often be aware of sensitive details in your clients' lives or businesses. Like any professional, you should never reveal these details to anyone, ever. Maintaining discretion will bring you credibility and trust and help you develop a sterling reputation.

3.3.4   Developing a "Thick Skin"

Inevitably, you're going to encounter clients who are particularly difficult to deal with. This is true of most service industries. You'll need to develop some skill in deflecting and defusing certain situations and client attitudes.

Holly Stiehl, a former hotel concierge and noted author and speaker to the hotel concierge industry, in an article entitled, "Customer Attitudes that Push Our Buttons," has divided problem clients into six basic personality types. (You can read the full article and more articles by this author at **www.thankyouverymuchinc.com/articles-videos/index.htm**.)

Based on Stiehl's experience, the six personality types are:

- The Entitled ("You owe me.")

- The Panicked ("But you promised!")

- The High and the Mighty ("Don't you know who I am?")

- The Bottom Liner ("Can you do this? Yes or no.")

- The Clueless ("If I go outside and it's raining, will I get wet?")

- The Imprisoned ("Nothing ever works out for me!")

It would be nice if we could lump all the "bad" clients under one of these categories and simply avoid them, but the truth is, even your best clients will exhibit traits or attitudes at times that push your buttons. Having a coping strategy will help you to better deal with even the most touchy clients.

It's important that you avoid a confrontational attitude if you feel that a client has treated you unfairly or disrespectfully (within limits, of course). Sometimes people are just stressed and need to vent, and you might happen to be on the receiving end. If you become defensive, the situation will merely escalate into a confrontation and you may end up losing a client.

Put yourself in the place of the client, and try to understand what may have motivated their behavior. Use empathy, instead of defensiveness. If you use language that lets clients know you are working with them and not against them, chances are they will take a less aggressive stance.

Here are some effective strategies for understanding how to defuse difficult situations:

- Identify your triggers

- Slow down your responses and remain calm

- Put yourself in the client's shoes (empathize)

- Listen effectively

- Always keep a positive, helpful attitude

This is all about customer service, of course. If you've never worked in a job with a customer service focus, this will be an important skill to develop. There are many seminars and workshops available to anyone wanting to learn or improve customer service skills.

Developing a Balance

You'll also need to develop (and maintain) a balance with each client between anticipating preferences and asking too many questions. And it will always be different. Some people are easy to please. "I would love it if I came home and my fridge was full of food — any food," confesses busy entrepreneur Stephen Beauchesne. "I don't have the time for or interest in making a shopping list," he explains.

Clients like Stephen are great, because they're not overly picky. Others will want to micromanage every step you take, until it feels like you have someone over your shoulder all the time. With these clients, building trust is very important. And it may take time to get there. Use your diplomacy and tact to get them to understand that you need some space to do your best work. The best way to build confidence in your skills is to find ways to exceed expectations every time.

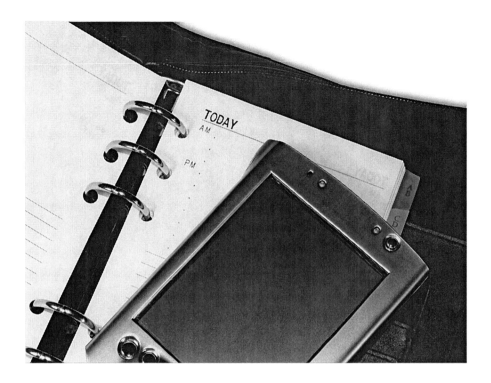

3.4 Organizational Skills

Organizational skills are important both to you personally in running your own business and to your clients who rely on you to put their lives in order. Being well organized will make your work much easier, especially if you have your own personal concierge business.

There will be times you'll have to juggle a number of tasks at the same time, such as meeting with clients, finding and purchasing items, scheduling things like hotel reservations or airline tickets, handling your finances, etc. You will have to keep track of paper work and ensure that everything is completed to your clients' satisfaction, on time and on budget.

3.4.1 Being Detail Oriented

Seeing the big picture is important, but you'll need to be able to break that vision into smaller pieces. If you remember the many tasks outlined in Chapter 2 that you might be called on to complete for clients, you can see that trying to keep track of everything could soon overwhelm you. On top of that, you'll need to stay up-to-date on all the administrative tasks involved in your job or business.

To track everything you do, consider using a task management tool. This might include either a day-timer, preferably with a single page devoted to one day, or scheduling software that you can use on your computer, iPhone, BlackBerry or PDA (personal digital assistant). Whatever way you choose to do it, be sure to set up a reminder system a day or two ahead of important events or tasks. You might also consider using a large visual organizer type of calendar where you can see everything at a glance for the coming month.

You could color-code blocks of time on a calendar with a highlighter pen that will help you organize your tasks for the week. For example, if you know that Tuesdays between 10:00 a.m. and 1:00 p.m. you usually spend meeting with store's buyers to see what will be coming in, block it in throughout your calendar and change it only in emergency situations. If you block in your "must do" activities ahead of time, you won't be tempted to accommodate clients in ways that cause you stress or a loss of valuable information (and you will have automatically limited the number of hours you will work).

In the beginning of your job or new business venture, you probably will put in some extra hours to learn the business and develop your clientele. However, those extra hours should be productive rather than representing too many entries into your calendar for you to handle everything you need to do just for the sake of taking on new clients. Remember that keeping your business organized is an important task that you will need to devote a certain number of hours to each week as well.

Another important area in which to be organized is your business finances, including bookkeeping, keeping track of receipts, filing any papers required for tax or licensing purposes, etc. (See Chapter 5 for more about these areas of running a business.) You may not be in the habit of keeping receipts for everything you purchase, but as a business owner, everything you spend money on to run your business is deductible for tax purposes. You'll need to have a paper trail for tax authorities in order to prove these expenses, so be sure to always ask for a receipt.

Once you have an organizational system in place, you will then find it easier to schedule tasks that go into keeping your clients happy.

3.4.2   Time Management

Time management skills are critical to being successful in this business. At times it may seem that there is never enough time to do everything that needs to be done for yourself and your clients. There are a number of ways that you can manage time more efficiently if it seems you never have enough of it:

Keep a time activity log, such as the one shown on the next page. For a few days, jot down things you're doing as you do them, and note the times when you change activities. After a few days, analyze the log. Chances are you will notice some time-wasters. To get real insight from this activity, make sure you don't change your normal behavior.

Another way to get control of your time is to concentrate on results, rather than just being busy. If you have ever had the experience of working hard but achieving little, it might be due to the "Pareto Principle," also known as the 80/20 rule. For most people, 20% of their activities lead to 80% of results. The other 80% of their time is spent at "busy work," doing something but getting less (20%) results.

Remember to do tasks that are most important first. To help you identify priority tasks think about the following four task rankings based on their urgency and importance:

- Urgent and important

- Non-urgent and important

- Urgent and non-important

- Non-urgent and non-important

While it might be logical to focus first on tasks that are both urgent and important, many people spend a lot of time on tasks that are not important, either because those tasks are urgent or because they are easier to complete. Completing a lot of easy tasks, even if they're non-important, can give people a sense of accomplishment. Of course, putting off the more difficult tasks that are important but non-urgent eventually leads to them becoming urgent.

Time Activity Log

	SUN	MON	TUE	WED	THU	FRI	SAT
A.M.							
12:00							
1:00							
2:00							
3:00							
4:00							
5:00							
6:00							
7:00							
8:00							
9:00							
10:00							
11:00							
P.M.							
12:00							
1:00							
2:00							
3:00							
4:00							
5:00							
6:00							
7:00							
8:00							
9:00							
10:00							
11:00							

Set daily goals to help keep you on track. For example, resolve to review your calendar first thing each morning so that you don't miss something or fall behind in something else. This will help you focus on what needs to be accomplished on any given day.

Divide your tasks into lists based on priorities. Your A-list should be things that must get done today. Your B-list is items to do only if everything on the A-list gets done (for example, errands that could be done tomorrow or the day following that). Your C-list is everything else that should be done only after everything on your A-list and B-list has been done.

TIP: Remember that priorities change over time. The A-B-C designations should be reviewed monthly to see if they still reflect your priorities.

Using this system will help you to control what happens in your day. You can use the Time Activity Log as a weekly planner. Start by filling the parts of your daily routine that are unavoidable, such as commuting, meetings (with clients, vendors, salespeople, etc.), or other scheduled events. Start filling in the blank time with A-list to-do items. When the A-list items are finished, move on the B-list and then eventually to the C-list. Once you have your own time under control, you will be in a much better position to manage other people.

3.5   Business Skills

Among the most important skills you will need if you're planning to start your own company are business skills or what many people generally call "business acumen." Many of the skills typically associated with other business ventures apply to the concierge business as well.

If you don't run a smart business, you won't be around to help your clients very long. Get to know where you stand financially, and regularly crunch the numbers to determine the best, most profitable use of your time. Learn to delegate, or even refer business away to other companies when necessary. If you have little or no experience with the day-to-day aspects of running the business side of a company, don't worry. Like other skills important for success, business skills can be learned, too.

Some of the skills most often associated with business owners are:

- Entrepreneurial

- Marketing

- Accounting

3.5.1 Entrepreneurial Skills

The online encyclopedia, Wikipedia, defines an entrepreneur as "a person who takes the risks involved to undertake a business venture. In doing so, they are said to efficiently and effectively use [their resources]." As a new business owner you probably already have the heart of an entrepreneur. If you didn't, you wouldn't be thinking about starting your own business.

Whether you come into this career from another job in a related industry like hospitality, or you've been a personal assistant, or come from some other line of work, you may have already been involved in some kind of entrepreneurial venture. But even if you've never owned a business before in your life, you can succeed as a personal concierge business owner through some basic entrepreneurial skills and efficient use of the resources available to you. These skills include "hard" skills like business planning, marketing, accounting and bookkeeping, as well as "soft" skills like determination, drive, and a will to succeed.

You probably already have the "soft" skills in your skills set, but if you feel you don't yet have the "hard" skills associated with entrepreneurship, don't worry. These can easily be developed. If you're already naturally a good communicator, good with people and well organized as explored in previous sections, you just have to learn more about the business aspects to round out your knowledge. In the meantime, you can take a short quiz at **www.bdc.ca/EN/advice_centre/benchmarking_tools/Pages/entrepreneurial_self_assessment.aspx** to see how well you fit into the entrepreneur mold.

One tool for helping you to focus on what's involved in being an entrepreneur is business planning. Section 4.2 looks in detail at how to develop a business plan to get your concierge business up and running by outlining and clarifying what your business will offer, deciding how you will finance your business, creating a market plan, etc. In addition to addressing these important business issues, a business plan will also help you to understand some of the other basic "hard" skills required of a business owner, such as marketing and accounting skills (discussed in further detail below).

Canada Business (**www.canadabusiness.ca**, click on "English" then on "Starting a Business") has a great deal of helpful information for anyone thinking of starting their own business. They offer the following tips to new entrepreneurs for identifying and creating a unique service:

- Take advantage of a market switch

- Capitalize on a growth trend

- Take advantage of new fashions or fads

- Cover market gaps or shortages

- Imitate a successful product or idea

- Transfer a concept from one industry to another

- Invent a new product or service

- Create a market demand

- Serve unique client groups

- Take advantage of circumstances

- Find people with under-used skills

As you can see from this list there are a great number of ways that you can make your business or services unique. Starting with the numerous suggestions in Chapter 2 for services you might offer to clients, the possibilities for creating a unique concierge business are almost endless.

For example, one Los Angeles concierge business saw a need for concierge services in apartment complexes that did not provide, or could not afford to provide, such services to their tenants. The company, Los Angeles Concierge Solutions, now offers a variety of services marketed to its clients through the management offices of the apartment complexes they live in. This is an example of identifying and taking advantage of a market gap (fourth bullet above).

Another example, capitalizing on a growth trend, is illustrated by the increasingly common trend of personal concierge companies offering their services as personal office assistants on an on-demand basis to smaller companies that need such services but can't afford to hire a full-time or even part-time personal assistant.

However you choose to create your own unique market niche, you will need to know some basic marketing skills to get your message out to potential clients. Once you have clients and your business is running you'll need to keep track of your everyday finances, including your income and expenses, and your assets, in order to monitor the success of your venture and keep track of taxes. Below, we'll look at each of these important areas and the skills you'll need to succeed in them.

3.5.2   Marketing Skills

Owning your own business always starts with making clients aware that you exist. This is true of absolutely every business and especially true in the personal concierge industry. You will be catering to a specific clientele, people who don't have the time or desire to do certain tasks themselves, and you'll need to let them know you are out there ready to help them with their problems.

Establishing yourself in any market is a three step approach. You will need to:

- Determine your market demographic (i.e. who are the people that need your services?)

- Find out who you are competing against within that demographic (your competitors)

- Figure out how you will make your target demographic aware of your services.

As mentioned in section 1.1.2, the typical customer for a majority of personal concierge business owners polled in the ICEA Future Watch study are people in their 30s and 40s who earn between $50,000 to $500,000 per year. This is an example of a market demographic (one based on income). Chances are, a single mother with three children who earns the national average of $31,000 or less is not going to have the extra cash needed to afford your services. It might be a mistake, then, to try to market to people in this income range.

To identify various demographics in your area, consider census statistics for where you live. These might include stats like the number of people in certain age groups, their earnings, types of occupations (for example, technical, labor, or professional), and other meaningful data like this. Try the U.S. Census Bureau website at **http://factfinder2. census.gov/faces/nav/jsf/pages/index.xhtml** (click on "Topics", then on "People"). In Canada try the Stats Canada website. The 2006 census page at **http://www12.statcan.gc.ca/census-recensement/2006/dp-pd/ prof/92-591/index.cfm?Lang=E** has the most complete data available free. Type in the name of your community in the Search box.

Another good resource for finding this kind of data is the website of the community you live in (either at the municipal or county level). Municipal and county government websites often have reports on various aspects of the local economy. Look for an "Economic Development" link or something similar. You can find free demographic information such as age, education and earnings, as well as economic development information, which will give you a good cross-section of the local population, level of education, what they earn, and who the major employers are.

There are other places to find relevant information, too. Check with tourist boards (numbers of vacationers who might need tickets for local events, etc.), pet industry organizations (for numbers and types of pets), your local Chamber of Commerce website, and so on. The Home-TownLocator.com and BestPlaces.net websites are also good sources of information about towns and cities across the U.S. Just type in the name of your community to find links to a wide range of facts and figures about it.

This is also a good time to check out the competition. Find out how many other personal concierge businesses are located in your area by searching the Yellow Pages and your local Chamber of Commerce website. You could also try a directory search at the International Concierge and Lifestyle Management Association website (**http://iclma.org/member_ directory**). Then, find out what services they offer by visiting their websites.

You should have a pretty good idea after researching your competitors whether or not your proposed services are a good fit with your target market. For example, if you were thinking about offering personal shopping services exclusively, but found that there were already 20 businesses in your area offering the same service, you might want to think about including other services as well. You can still offer personal shopping of course, but just be prepared for the fact that you'll get a smaller share of business in that service area than in another service offering that isn't as well covered by competitors.

Once you know the population and economic characteristics of your area and who your competitors are, you can start to think about the services you would like to include as part of your business. This will mean deciding on ways to reach whatever slice of the population you think will want your services. This might include using marketing techniques like advertising, sending out a press release, etc.

You'll need marketing tools such as business cards, brochures, and a website, all of which can help you reach your target demographic. Since a lot of new business in this industry comes by referrals and word of mouth, you'll want to think about ways to network to help you gain additional exposure. In Chapter 6 we'll look at a variety of marketing ideas to help you get your services known to potential clients.

3.5.3   Accounting Skills

In terms of the long-term success of your business, few aspects are more important than the day-to-day accounting and bookkeeping skills required to keep everything running smoothly. While you don't have to be a professional accountant to run a business, you will find that having a good working knowledge of how your accounting system works will be a big advantage to you.

Many businesses hire professional accountants to organize and monitor their accounting system and keep their books up to date. If you have a background in accounting or bookkeeping then you may choose to do your own books and just use a professional's services for the "big picture" aspects. This would include having an accountant calculate and submit tax returns, help you with long-term planning and so on.

Alternatively, if you don't have any experience in this aspect of your business, you might choose to hire a bookkeeper, perhaps on a part-time basis. You would still have a professional accountant look after your quarterly (every three months) or year-end returns. Bookkeeping services are relatively inexpensive compared to the services of a professional accountant and well worth the money if you don't have the experience or desire to handle this part of running your business.

Most community colleges offer basic accounting and bookkeeping courses if you do want to learn how to do your own bookkeeping. Even if you would rather hire a bookkeeper, you should still learn at least the basics so that you will know what your bookkeeper and your accountant are talking about. You can learn more about how to find accounting courses in the next chapter. We'll also take a more in-depth look at how to implement accounting procedures in your own business in section 4.4.

3.6   Informal Learning

3.6.1   Learning a Little Bit of Everything

A personal concierge is expected to know a little bit about everything, and hopefully have a few areas of in-depth expertise as well. While learning "everything" may sound like a daunting task, most requests will fall into similar categories and you'll build your skills over time. According to personal concierge Dustyn Shroff, "a lot of what we do on a daily basis is not something in which we may be experts, but that's not to say we can't become experts!" Books, the Internet, magazines, and short workshops or courses at your community college will help you with:

- Basic computer troubleshooting

- Basic home repair

- Etiquette knowledge

- Household management

- Office skills (typing, shipping parcels, etc.)

- Organization strategies

- Party planning

- Pet care and/or childcare

- Personal chef or home cooking

- Selecting flowers and wine

- Small business and entrepreneurial issues

- Technology (cell phones, PDAs, iPods, etc.)

- Travel planning

You'll find more tips below for informal ways of learning about some of these areas. You should also spend some time getting to know as much as you can about your city or region. Pick up brochures from the tourist bureau, or join the Chamber of Commerce. Subscribe to the local newspaper, and make reading it part of your daily routine. If you don't know the city well, spend a few days driving around with map in hand to see the sights.

Online, one of the best peer-to-peer resources is Personal Assistant Pro. Members share ideas in a forum moderated by a working personal concierge, and more than 250 articles on personal concierge/personal assistant work are archived online. Membership is $25 to register and $10 monthly. Yahoo also has a group dedicated to errand services, accessible for free with selective membership.

- *Personal Assistant Pro*
  www.personalassistantpro.com

- *Yahoo Errand Services: A group for those with "time" to sell*
  http://finance.groups.yahoo.com/group/errand_services

In Chapter 2 we looked at some of the many services that you might offer to your clients. There are lots of informal ways to learn aspects of each of those services. Some may even give you opportunities to earn while you learn. We offer a few of these below, provided by experts we have interviewed in each of these areas. Note that you can read more about some of the learning methods mentioned, like finding a mentor, volunteering, and information interviews in more depth later in this section.

Home Organizing

- Check out the member pages at the Professional Organizers Web Ring (**www.organizerswebring.com**)

- Hire a professional organizing coach/mentor

- Check out the resources on the National Association of Professional Organizers website (**www.napo.net**)

- Contact a professional organizer in your area for an information interview

- Read as many books as you can about the many different kinds of organizing

Pet sitting

- Read books and magazines geared to pet lovers (there are all kinds, devoted to birds, cats, dogs, reptiles, even bugs)

- Work part-time or volunteer for:

  - SPCA or Humane Society

  - Local animal sanctuary

  - Pet groomers

  - Pet and pet supplies stores

  - Kennels

  - Veterinary clinics

  - Doggie daycare

- Own a pet so you know what the demands are

- Offer to pet-sit for family and friends for free

Personal Shopping

"You should know 'stuff,' like top designers for jewelry and clothing, and what festival is coming up, and where to buy narrow-sized shoes. Go and study areas of shops, and pay attention to selection and price and brands. That way, when you get a client who asks you where to find a hand-painted tie, you can say, 'I just saw some at a boutique in Birmingham. What's your favorite color?' Also, know your geographical areas beyond what your GPS can do for you."

— Personal Concierge Jill Burstein

Here are some ways to get to know "stuff" about personal shopping:

- Read consumer publications of all kinds

- Check out online department and specialty store catalogs

- Read retail and gift industry publications

- Observe other personal shoppers

- Get a part-time or full-time job at a retail or department store

- Window shop frequently to watch for new trends

- Check out retailers on the Internet (**www.ecr.ryerson.ca/retailers. html**)

Travel Planning

Here are some informal ways to learn more about travel planning:

- Become familiar with world geography (use an atlas, Google Earth, etc.)

- Do some traveling

- Watch TV shows on Discovery Travel Channel, CTV Travel, OLN, etc.

- Check out the Travel Pulse website (**www.travelpulse.com**)

- Contact tourism offices to find out information about various destinations

- Work as a tour organizer or group leader

- Volunteer at a local tourist destination (museum, gallery, local attraction)

- Work with a travel supplier (airline, cruise, etc.) as a booking agent

- Make travel arrangements for friends and family for free

- Become a referral agent for a travel agency and drum up business for them for a small commission

- Work the front desk or reservations line for a local hotel or rental car company

- Read trade publications

Event and Party Planning

There are lots of great sites on the Internet where you can find event and party planning resources. You will likely find experts in your locality with whom you can consult to learn more. Here are some additional tips for learning about this aspect of your business.

- Set up an information interview with vendors like caterers, florists, venue coordinators, etc.

- Interview a professional event planner, party planner or wedding planner

- Job shadow a professional event planner (spend a day, week or other limited period observing them at work)

- Evaluate events (take note of registration process, logistics, organization, etc.)

- Volunteer to assist at an event (for example, a charity event)

- Plan an event for free for family and friends

- Read trade magazines like *Event Solutions Magazine* and *Special Events Magazine*

- Check out websites such as **www.meetings-conventions.com**

- Visit websites like **www.party411.com** or **www.partypop.com** for ideas

Child Care

- Volunteer or work part-time at a local daycare (community centers, YMCA/YWCA, church, etc.), school, or library (many offer children's programs)

- Volunteer with other children's programs in your area (check your local volunteer agencies for opportunities)

- Have good knowledge of needs of various age groups, hygiene, nutrition, age-appropriate activities, how to cope with emergencies

- Take an ECE training program

- Take first aid and CPR courses

These are just some of the ways that you can learn a variety of skills you will find helpful at little or no cost to you. You might even make money doing it. Below we'll look at some additional ways to get information directly from experts who already work in this career, so that you can learn from the valuable experiences of someone who has "been there."

3.6.2   Information Interviews

An information interview is defined as a brief meeting with someone who is working in a career you are interested in learning about. The goal of the information interview is to collect information that will allow you to make informed decisions about your career as a personal concierge.

The personal and professional benefits of an information interview are numerous:

- Help expand your professional network

- Increase your confidence

- Gain access to the most up-to-date career information

- Identify your strengths and weaknesses

- Get a look at the business from the inside

To arrange information interviews, start with your network of contacts, including family and friends, to ask if they know anyone working as a personal concierge or possibly have used the services of a personal concierge and could help you connect. If possible, go beyond getting a name and telephone number. Ask if they would get in touch with people they know in the industry to see if you can contact them to ask a few questions.

If no one in your network knows anyone who works in this business, you can try to arrange meetings by making cold calls. First do some research to come up with a list of local personal concierges who work in your area of interest or specialization(s). The more research you do prior to an interview, the more efficient it will be and the better impression you will leave.

You can find personal concierges who belong to the International Concierge and Lifestyle Management Association at **http://iclma.org/member_directory**. To find other small personal concierge companies, consult your Yellow Pages under "Personal Concierge Services" or your local Chamber of Commerce for any listed in your area.

Once you have selected some local businesses, it becomes a matter of picking up the phone and calling. Large and small firms will often have receptionists or administrative assistants answering the phones. They can be a valuable source of contact information. Ideally, you want to reach a senior person and directly ask them for a meeting.

Although you are conducting an "information interview," it is usually better to avoid using that term when you first call. Many professionals assume someone who wants to set up an information interview is actually looking for a job, not simply looking to learn about the profession. So they may decline to meet with you if they do not have any current job openings.

Instead, it may be better to say that you are doing research and politely ask if you can arrange to meet with them for 20 minutes to learn about the career. People are much more likely to agree to a meeting if they know it won't take too much time. However, others in the business say that it's not unreasonable to suggest a lunch-hour meeting.

It's important to remember that while some people are generous with their time and encouraging to newcomers, others may simply be too busy to meet with everyone who wants career advice. Anyone who works in a career field that many people are trying to break into may be inundated with requests for information interviews every week. If someone you contact says they don't have time for a meeting, politely ask if they know anyone who might be available to talk with you.

If someone agrees to a meeting, arrive on time and come prepared with a list of questions such as the following:

- How did you get started as a personal concierge?

- What do you wish you had known when you were first getting into this business?

- What are typical duties in your job?

- Based on a quick review of my experience to date, what training or experience do you think I should pursue next?

- What advice do you have for someone just getting started?

If you have agreed to meet for a limited time, such as 20 minutes, let the interviewee know when the time limit is up, say you know they're busy, and offer to leave. If they are willing to continue that's fine, but don't stay longer without permission. Thank them for their time and any referrals they were able to provide. After the meeting, send a thank you note to the person you met with and, if someone referred you, thank that person as well.

> **TIP:** Ideally, an information interview should be a face-to-face meeting, but if this can't be arranged a telephone interview still has benefits. You may even get valuable advice from someone who isn't available to talk but is willing to answer questions by email.

3.6.3   Finding a Mentor

A mentor is someone who has experienced the same challenges you will be facing as a beginning personal concierge. They have learned their lessons the hard way, and are willing to save you time and effort by showing you how to do things right the first time.

A mentor is also someone who is willing to give you personal training and advice either for free, for money or for an exchange of services. Informal networking is a great way to start off building relationships with people who can help you along in your career. While developing these relationships, you will likely come across some people who are extra friendly, extra helpful, or just someone you click with right away. These people are likely candidates for being willing to take the relationship to a more personal level and become a mentor to you.

> **TIP:**   Ideally your mentor will be working successfully as a concierge themselves, so that they can share with you the "how to" instead of just the "how not to."

While books and certification programs for personal concierges will get you so far, the great thing about a mentor is that their advice is up-to-the-minute, personalized to your situation, and interactive—as in "you ask, they tell." And if you play your cards right, you could have a person to turn to for help making career-related decisions for years to come.

If you can't find a mentor in your area who has their own personal concierge business, consider mentoring with someone who comes from a related industry. This might be someone working in the hospitality industry, such as a hotel concierge or someone otherwise involved in guest services. Other options might be working with a variety of other experts with experience related to the services you wish to offer in your own personal concierge business (see section 3.6.1 for more about finding opportunities like these).

Another good resource to try to find a mentor for business startup is SCORE at **www.score.org**. They will match you with someone in your area who can help you in your business start-up process.

How to Approach a Potential Mentor

If you don't identify a suitable mentor in your early networking, you may need to start looking more aggressively. An excellent way to connect with professionals in the industry is to visit them where they work, if possible.

Especially when you are planning on starting a business, it's actually to your advantage to approach a mentor who is not in the same town as you so that they know you won't be competing for the same clients. Also, being more wide-ranging in your choice gives you the opportunity to look for true experts in the field, as opposed to connecting solely on the basis of who is located nearby.

To make the most of your relationship, look for a mentor who, as much as possible, shares your intended specialty areas (Chapter 2 outlines the various specialty areas you might choose from), your values, and your way of doing business. If you can't find all this in one person, you may want to approach more than one mentor to round out the advice you receive.

Once you have identified one or a few potential mentors, approach them with a written letter or email of introduction. Or you can use these same notes as conversation points when you meet with them for coffee or lunch.

Explain why you selected them as a potential mentor. This may be their success within specialty areas you are interested in or it may be that you admire their skills. Whatever your reason, let your potential mentor know why you chose them from among all the professionals you might have contacted.

Make a specific request. Rather than just saying you want them to be your mentor, explain what you are asking for. Do you want to talk with them on the telephone once a week for 20 minutes? Do you want to meet with them once a month over lunch? Do you want to communicate with them on a weekly basis by email? Also, be open to their offer of an alternative method of contact, since you are the one asking for a favor. Some people shy away from mentoring because they fear it will take too much time or energy. Assure your potential mentor this isn't the case.

Offer something in return. While some professional mentors charge a fee for mentoring (see below), others will provide the service at no charge. However, there may be many demands on their time, so think about what you can offer back to them. A free lunch is a start, but it's better to volunteer your services or share information. Maybe you are a great writer and can offer to write your mentor's next brochure or newsletter, for example.

If they are located reasonably close to you, you could propose an unpaid internship where you would help out in your mentor's office on a part-time basis at no charge to them. This can be a win-win for both of you — they benefit from your help while you learn from their experience.

Mentoring for a Fee

If it's not possible to connect with a mentor in person, you can look for suitable professionals on the Internet using a search engine like Google or an association directory like the one at the ICLMA website (mentioned in the previous section), or in the Yellow Pages under "Personal Concierge Services." You may find it faster to look for someone who is already working as a mentor rather than approach people who may be unfamiliar or unreceptive to the idea. Again, this comes down to which you have more of: time or money.

In the case where you are paying a mentor, you need to make sure you are getting value for your money. Ask lots of questions up front about their specialty and what their availability will be like, and ask if you can speak to other people they have mentored to ensure they were satisfied with the results.

TIP: Your mentor should be currently working as a personal concierge or in a related industry, or else they may be out of touch with today's market. If you have any doubts, keep shopping around until you find someone who has the right credentials and reliability.

3.7 Getting Some Experience

Hands-on experience is a great way to build your skills quickly. If you can spare the time, a short stint in a hospitality-related environment can open your eyes to great customer service, and what is expected of those who are hired to help.

"Tapping into your own personal experiences in being extremely busy and needing help, researching the industry, and talking to other concierges are my suggestions in preparing yourself," says Delmar Johnson of The Concierge Place.

Other personal concierge services in the area may be willing to let you tag along, or run some basic errands for their clients. You are likely to find some resistance if you express your intention to open a competing service, as mentioned earlier, but if the concierge is truly busy they may be relieved to have someone to refer overflow clients to in the near future.

"I have had several ride-alongs who are local and want to know how I run my business on a daily basis. I say, 'Hop in.' I would love to fall back on a quality concierge service to take care of my clients, so why not show them how I do it? I could learn a thing or two from them as well, I am sure," says personal concierge Jill Burstein.

3.7.1 Volunteer Experience

Below, you will find a number of helpful suggestions for finding volunteer opportunities. You can find additional suggestions in section 3.6.1.

Friends and Family

One way to get hands-on concierge experience is to offer your services free of charge to friends and family members. For example, you could set up a schedule for running errands, providing friends and family with a set number of errands you will run for them. This will give you some experience in setting up a client database, coordinating multiple tasks, and get you some feedback about how well you performed the work.

When a friend or family member wants to use your personal concierge services, try to treat them the way you would treat a "real" client. Schedule a meeting with them and go through every stage of the service process. This will include each of the following tasks (Chapter 5 explains these in detail):

- Do an initial consultation
- Gather information about the client (important issues, personal/family profile)
- Conduct a needs assessment
- Sign a letter of engagement with the client
- Sign a services agreement with the client
- Submit an invoice

A key part of evaluating the service delivery process is getting client feedback. A couple of things you can ask your family and friend "clients" are if they thought the service was valuable to them and what they would be willing to pay for it. Also, assuming they're happy with the experience, ask them for a letter of recommendation or testimonial about you and your services. Every time you perform services for someone, even if it's a friend or a family member (preferably with a different last name from yours), ask for a letter of recommendation.

When you're ready to move on from friends and family, ask for referrals to people they know who might be interested in trying your service for free for one week. You may end up with some regular clients this way, but at the very least you will have references for your first paying clients or testimonials to use in your marketing materials as you build your clientele. (Additional advice on getting outstanding testimonials is explored in section 6.4.3.)

Non-Profit Organizations

Another way you can get practical experience is by volunteering your services to local non-profit organizations and community associations. You'll get the benefit of helping a worthy cause while you hone your skills, plus volunteering can be an excellent way to make contacts which could lead to future employment opportunities.

Assuming your goal is to get experience related to your personal concierge business and services, you should leave non-relevant tasks to other volunteers. Instead, be sure to volunteer to work at tasks that will help you learn more about the specific areas you're interested in.

Another option may be to offer your company's services on a pro bono basis (i.e. free of charge). For example, a local animal shelter might be happy to have someone to walk their dogs for them or a big corporation in your area might need some help buying holiday gifts in conjunction with local charitable organizations. Whatever your specialty, chances are there is an organization in your area that would be willing to use your services.

The best approach to offering your services is to try to arrange a meeting with the executive director of the non-profit organization. You would gather information about the organization's needs and present a proposal to provide relevant services. If this can't be arranged, call and get your message to the most senior people you can. Ask them what's the best way for you to send the proposal. (See section 6.7.2 for a sample proposal for services.)

In some cases, volunteer organizations seek out the help of service providers through advertising or RFPs. Hundreds of volunteer opportunities are posted at **www.volunteermatch.org** seeking help in a variety of areas. Recent posts included volunteers needed for puppy/dog walking, gala event assistance, office assistants, and many more. If you can't find anything posted for your locality, you might propose something similar to a non-profit organization in your community.

You can find help in locating your community's non-profit groups through the Internet. GuideStar is a searchable database of more than 1.8 million IRS-recognized non-profit organizations in the United States. Visit **www2.guidestar.org** then click on "Advanced Search" to search by your city or state. CharityVillage has a similar database of Canadian non-profits at **www.charityvillage.com** (after you click on "Enter," click on "Links to NPOs"). You might also contact your local Volunteer Center or Chamber of Commerce. Both of these organizations usually run a volunteer matching program and can help provide the information you need to get involved.

Whatever volunteer opportunities you choose to take advantage of, make sure to ask for referrals and testimonials, and get permission to use satisfied clients as references.

3.7.2   Internships

Some of the larger concierge businesses as well as resorts and hotels offer internships for concierges and personal assistants. An internship is a great way to get valuable experience in an area you would like to specialize in. Though often internships are unpaid, some internships are paid or offer a small stipend. As an intern, you will be trained in the same way as a paid employee and will do many of the same tasks.

The purpose of working as an intern is for you to get experience, while the company you work for gets your services in return for the training they give you. Just as you would with applying for a regular job, you'll need a resume and cover letter and you'll go through an interview process, in most cases.

To see an example of the qualifications required and a job description for one concierge internship position, visit the Eur-Am Center website at **www.eurabbey.com/students/internships.html**. The Eur-Am Center offers a concierge internship at a hotel. Check out the position at **www. provisionsfr.ws/InternshipsinEurope/Concierge/tabid/3475/Default. aspx**.

To see an example of an internship opportunity at a large concierge company visit **www.planit-ec.com/contactUs.php**. You can also check out sites like **www.internweb.com** (free registration required) to search for internships. To find other internships try typing "concierge internship" or "hospitality internship" into a search engine like Google.

3.8   Professional Associations & Training

Although there is nothing about being a personal concierge that requires formal training, getting ideas from other service providers at courses or conferences can be a great boost to your business. Alternately, any hospitality or household management courses, especially butler training, can be a helpful leg up in the industry.

3.8.1   Professional Associations

Here are a few professional organizations that offer support or training to their members. Clients will feel more confident in your service level and professionalism if they can see you are certified by a professional association with standards of excellence. If there is no local chapter of a professional association in your region, consider starting up your own.

National Concierge Association

The National Concierge Association (**www.nationalconciergeassociation. com**) is a network of professional concierges and vendors, with members across North America and elsewhere in the world. They sponsor an annual national conference, which is held in a different U.S. city each year. Past conferences have been held in places like Las Vegas, New Orleans, San Jose, and Newport, Rhode Island. A variety of educational seminars are offered at the conferences featuring subjects like marketing, business strategies, use of technology, and more. To become a member, you need to be working as a personal assistant or concierge and prove that this is your paid profession.

International Concierge and Lifestyle Management Association

Like the NCA, the ICLMA (**http://iclma.org**) is a networking association that includes concierge and vendor members with hundreds of members in over 24 countries. You can join ICLMA as a "Regular Member" for $150. You'll be listed in the membership directory, and will have access to a members library, social networking groups, a certification program and other resources.

The ICLMA holds an annual conference for its members. Seminars are generally focused on the needs of those already in business, however new members are always welcome to attend. Past educational topics at the conference have included niche marketing, general marketing strategies, personal shopping services, various business topics, and so on.

3.8.2   Training and Education

Training programs are also available from the following. The first focuses on concierge training while the others focus on household management and personal assistant training.

> **Note:**   The training courses listed are neither endorsed nor audited by the author or FabJob. Only you can decide what training, if any, is right for you.

Les Clefs d'Or

This prestigious and venerable organization (**www.lcdusa.org**), whose name translates as "The Golden Keys," was founded in the 1920s in France, and represents professional hotel concierges worldwide. They have some 3,000 members in 39 countries. To become a member you need to be employed by a hotel as a concierge for a minimum of three years. Credit of one year's employment is given if you are a graduate of a recognized professional concierge training program. Non-hotel concierge work experience does not count as a qualification for membership. New members must provide a resume and cover letter to their regional chapters when applying for membership.

Les Clefs d'Or association holds a number of "Congresses" each year in various locations around the world. A Pan American Congress is held every second year, with the next one scheduled for Las Vegas, Nevada, in 2012. At each national Congress a special educational symposium is held for the benefit of members. In addition, the Congress provides educational programs with a number of colleges and universities in the U.S., networking opportunities, open forum discussions and sales and marketing discussions.

Errand and Concierge Service University

Program Type:	Concierge training
Location:	Across the U.S. (check website for locations and schedule)
Format:	Onsite seminars, webinars, and at-home training
Cost:	$200-$525, depending on program
Contact:	(951) 427-6067
Website:	**www.ecsuniversitytraining.com**

Professional Domestic Institute

Program Type:	One year programs in household management/butler, administrative household management, personal assistant
Location:	67 Clairedan Drive Powell, OH 43065

Format:	Home study
Cost:	$3,900 (includes online support, course materials, text books, etc.)
Contact:	(740) 881-3358
Website:	**www.worldclassservice.net/index2.htm** or **www.housestaff.net/ahm.asp**

The International Institute of Modern Butlers

Program Type:	Private Residence or Hotel/Hospitality Butler course
Location:	411 Cleveland Street #234 Clearwater, FL 33755
Format:	Correspondence course
Cost:	$2,500
Contact:	(813) 354-2734
Website:	**www.modernbutlers.com/html/ butler-correspondence-course-1.html**

Magnums Butler

Program Type:	Butler and Personal Concierge training
Location:	8 Parkhaven Close, Coes Creek, Queensland 4560, Australia
Format:	Online course or on-site training in Australia
Cost:	Lessons 1-10 can be purchased for AUD$125-$170 per course, or the entire program for AUD$1,325
Website:	**www.magnumsbutlers.com**

In addition to the courses listed above, look for advertised local workshops and seminars in your area. Many local venues offer workshops and seminars in topics like shopping, event planning, organizing, etc., which can be helpful as you develop your skills and knowledge.

To learn more about business and entrepreneurial subjects, try a continuing education course from your local community college. To find a college offering programs in basic bookkeeping, entrepreneurship, accounting, courses in customer service, and other business-related topics, check out **www.petersons.com** or **www.schoolfinder.com** (Canada). Many colleges also offer these types of courses by correspondence (distance learning) or online.

4. Starting a Concierge Business

Starting up your own business will be simultaneously one of the most exhilarating and terrifying things you'll ever do. Your best strategy is to go in with a plan. In this chapter we'll look at some of the issues you'll need to address as you start to formulate and refine your unique business concept.

This chapter is designed to help you make decisions about the issues you will face in starting your business. (The next chapter will help you decide how to market your business to attract clients.) It begins with some start-up considerations then looks at how to create a business plan and continues with an overview of other factors you'll need to consider in starting your own business.

4.1 Start-up Considerations

4.1.1 Starting Full-Time or Part-Time

If you are currently employed, some of the questions you may need to consider are:

- Should I quit my job and start my concierge business on a full-time basis?

- Should I remain at my current job and start my business on the side?

- Would my employer let me keep my job on a part-time basis so I could be available to meet with clients during business hours and have a secure source of income while I'm getting my business off the ground?

- If I leave my job to start my own business would my current employer possibly become one of my clients?

While some of your choices will depend on external factors such as whether or not your employer allows employees to moonlight, other choices will be yours to make.

Here are some other start-up decisions you should consider.

Other Start-Up Decisions

Whether or not you are currently employed, there are many other decisions you will face when starting your business. You'll find additional information in this chapter and the chapters following to help you in making decisions like:

- Should I have a specialization or offer general life concierge services?

- How much should I invest in start-up costs?

- Should I incorporate?

- Should I work with one or more partners?

- How should I set up my office?

- What should I name my company?

- What business systems do I need to set up (e.g. for invoicing)?

- Should I hire support staff?

- What types of insurance should I get?

- What fees should I charge?

4.1.2 Start-Up Expenses

Expenses to Expect

So, how much is it going to cost you to start up a personal concierge business, anyway? That all depends on the equipment you already have on hand, and the services you want to provide. Assuming you will work out of your home and won't be leasing or purchasing office space, the biggest variable is whether or not you need to purchase or lease a vehicle.

Transportation

If you plan on transporting clients as part of your service, or if you don't have a reliable car, you may need to invest in something roomier, or at least something you can count on to start every morning. With gas prices being what they are, a fuel-efficient vehicle is a wise choice. Vehicle insurance is another consideration. If you already have a vehicle suitable for your needs, and you won't be driving clients, then all you do is add business-use to your insurance policy.

Electronic Equipment

The electronic equipment you use to do your job may include a computer, word processing and accounting software, a cell phone, fax machine, PDA, GPS, office printer, and a digital camera. It's likely that you have a few of these items already. If not, you'll need to invest some money to get properly outfitted. A laptop is a particularly useful investment if you have the available cash.

Other Expenses

After the vehicle and electronics, your other big costs will be website and/or graphic design, initial marketing expenses like business cards, brochures and vehicle signage, and setting up your business insurance. You will also have legal and accounting costs, and probably office furniture and supplies to buy.

> TIP: Always trade professional services where possible to cut your costs. See if your lawyer or accountant will take payment in concierge hours instead of cash, for example.

One major ongoing expense for your personal concierge business will be gas for your vehicle. Keep an eye on the fluctuations in price, and make sure that you set your fees high enough to withstand minor fluctuations. Major fluctuations may require raising your prices. As you'll read in section 5.2 on setting fees, most personal concierges charge back to the client any mileage after a basic amount.

Covering Expenses

In addition to budgeting enough cash to cover these expenses, you'll want to have some leeway with money you can use to front expenses for clients until you get paid. A line of credit works well, or you can have money banked for this purpose. If you use a line of credit, you'll need to add interest payments to your list of expenses too. Stay away from high-interest credit cards, if possible, unless you plan to pay off the balance within 30 days. This kind of debt can quickly add up to a big burden.

If your personal concierge business will be your primary source of income, you might want to have at least six months' living expenses (rent, mortgage, etc.) and business working capital (to cover business operating expenses) tucked away before you go at it full time. A year's worth is even better. This way you have time to build your business up to a level that will support you. This might be a good reason to consider going part-time in the beginning while you build up your savings.

And if you have a "day job" you should consider hanging on to it as long as you can. "When I started, I was still working full time," confesses personal concierge Jill Burstein. "I was terrified I would get a client, as I might have had to call off work!" she laughs. Whether you start full time or part time the expenses will be essentially the same in the end, and creating a start-up budget will help you to get a handle on your initial costs.

4.1.3   Budgeting for Start-Up Expenses

Let's take a closer look at the foreseeable costs involved in launching your business, so that you can quickly and easily calculate your start-up budget. You should keep your initial expenses as lean as possible. After you have some cash flow from your first clients, you can buy the extras that were not in the original budget.

A start-up worksheet has been included at the end of this section to help simplify the process. Once you've researched how much each item will cost, fill in those amounts and total up your starting budget. The overall amount will largely depend on what items you already own.

Here are some of the foreseeable start-up expenses you should expect:

- Business banking account and checks

- Business license and registration: While the fees shouldn't be too large, they should be added to the start-up budget.

- Business phone line and answering service

- Office equipment, packing materials, and supplies (see section 4.5 for more about setting up your office)

- Internet service

- Marketing and advertising: This includes building and hosting your website, networking costs to attend luncheons or meetings, and any paid advertising activity such as print advertisements, radio and TV spots, etc. (see Chapter 6 for more about marketing)

- Legal or accounting fees: If you will need the counsel of an attorney, accountant, or bookkeeper, this expenditure should be estimated and taken into account.

- Insurance: The minimum you need is liability insurance. As mentioned in section 4.3.2, you may also need to add in costs for health, disability or other insurance, if you need these policies.

- Living expenses: Since you won't have a steady paycheck as an entrepreneur, it is crucial that you save up about three to six months worth of living expenses, especially if you have no other sources of income to draw on while you build your business.

- Business working capital: Just like living expenses, you should start with enough money to fund your business for at least three to six months. This basically covers your costs to run the operation (supplies, phones, etc.) until you can use business revenue to pay the bills.

- Small inventory of gifts and cards

- Training: Any programs or workshops in which you enroll should be added into the budget. In some cases, training may end up being one of the top expenses. There are also small business classes or continuing education classes that you may decide to take.

- Professional memberships

- Wardrobe upgrade

4.1.4   Start-Up Financing

The initial start-up budget is one component of your business plan (see section 4.1.3) that you will want to create first. After you work out your start-up budget, you'll know if there's any need for investors or loans. A major benefit to working in this field is the low amount needed to get started as a business owner. In general, service businesses are cheaper to launch than businesses that sell products, because there is no inventory to buy and no retail location to open.

As discussed in Chapter 3, a training program or workshop can have its rewards, but it will also have an enrollment fee. If you decide this is the right path for you, be sure to include tuition and other training related costs in your start-up budget. Be sure to add association membership fees as well.

Sample Start-Up Expense Worksheet

Advertising/Marketing	$_____
Association fees	$_____
Bookkeeping fees	$_____
Business cards and printing	$_____
Computer/Printer/Fax/Copier	$_____
Insurance	$_____
Internet	$_____
Legal fees	$_____
Licenses and permits	$_____
Living expenses (3-6 months)	$_____
Misc. expenses (e.g. new wardrobe)	$_____
Office furniture costs (desk, file cabinet)	$_____
Office supplies	$_____
Other equipment and supplies	$_____
Telephone	$_____
Training and education	$_____
Utilities	$_____
Vehicle (Fuel & Maintenance)	$_____
Vehicle (Purchase or Lease)	$_____
Working capital (3-6 months)	$_____
Total Expenses	$_____
Minus Available Start-up Capital	$_____
Total Amount Needed	$_____

Financing Considerations

Depending on how you set up your business, start-up costs might range from almost nothing to thousands of dollars. Obviously, your start-up expenses will be much higher if you decide to rent space and buy office equipment.

You will also need to consider your "working capital" requirements. This is the money you will need for day-to-day operations. But, as mentioned earlier, there are the other expenses that will come out of your pocket before you get your first client—such as business cards, telephone, etc.

Many entrepreneurs are optimistic about how much money they will earn from their new businesses, and how quickly they will earn it. While you may be tremendously successful right from the start and exceed your own expectations, you should also be prepared for the possibility that it may take longer than expected for your business to earn enough to support you.

Depending on the start-up costs you calculate in your business plan, you may find you have all the money you need to get started in your savings account (or available elsewhere). If your own resources won't cover all the things you would like to do, you will need to look for outside financing.

Financing Options

Personal Savings

Evaluate your bank accounts, retirement plans, and investments for available funds to finance your new venture. Who better to borrow from than yourself? You might pay penalties for withdrawing funds early from certain plans and investments, but it keeps you from accumulating excessive debt.

Family

One place to look for financing is from family members. They may be willing to invest in your company or give you a loan to help you get started. To avoid any misunderstandings, it's wise to get any agreements in writing even with family members.

Moonlighting

You could always keep your day job and work as a personal concierge in the evening and on weekends, or you can downgrade to a part-time position and run your business with the extra time. This allows you to safely test being your own boss, while still having the shelter of a steady paycheck and benefits. Continuing to earn a salary of some kind to help cover your living expenses will also help keep your start-up costs down.

Credit Cards

Using plastic to finance a business should generally be avoided because of the potential for extremely high interest rates. However, if you've exhausted all of the other options, then this is something to think about using carefully. There are also lines of credit that can be obtained from various other lenders which give you access to a pre-approved loan amount as you need it.

Banks and Credit Unions

Another place to secure a small business loan is through a conventional bank, credit union, or other lender. If you decide to give this a try, you'll need a comprehensive and professional business plan in order to impress the loan officer.

If you decide to approach a bank for a business loan, be prepared. Write a loan proposal that includes detailed information about your business, how much money you want to borrow, what you plan to do with the money, and so on.

Some good advice about financing can be found at the websites listed below. Look into the Small Business Administration business assistance programs. The SBA has a Loan Guarantee Program that provides loans to small businesses. A similar program is available in Canada.

- *SBA: Financing*
  **www.sba.gov/category/navigation-structure/
  starting-managing-business/starting-business/
  preparing-your-finances**

- *Industry Canada: Small Business Financing Program*
  www.ic.gc.ca/eic/site/csbfp-pfpec.nsf/eng/Home

- *Nolo.com Resource Center*
  (Click on "Business, LLCs & Corporations, then on "Business Plans & Financing")
  www.nolo.com

4.1.5   Your Earning Needs

To calculate your earning needs, you'll need to figure out your monthly costs of doing business. Section 4.4.2 shows you how to chart your monthly and yearly cash flow (revenues and expenses).

After you chart your monthly expenses, add the amount of pay you want to take home in a month. Finally, divide that figure by the number of days in a month you want to work. The figure you're left with is the daily amount you need to earn to take home what you desire.

Sample Calculation		
Monthly costs		$1,250.00
Monthly salary	+	$2,500.00
Total	=	$3,750.00
Days to work/mo.	÷	15 days
Daily income must be:	=	$250.00

In the above calculation, the personal concierge would need to earn $250 a day to meet his or her financial goals. If it seemed unlikely that $250 a day was possible based on the local market conditions, then he or she could a) increase the number of days worked, b) lower salary expectations, or c) find ways to cut costs. For example, the same concierge would only need to earn $150 a day if he or she worked 25 days a month.

Your earnings are also dependent on the number (and sometimes the type) of clients you have. From the example calculation, the personal concierge needed to earn $250 per day for 15 days each month in order to meet earning needs. The average hourly rate of earnings for a concierge in North America is about $40 per hour (see section 5.2, Setting Your Fees). This would represent roughly six hours' work in the example above. Depending on the types of services you offer and where you live, you may earn more or less than the national average, and you may therefore need more or fewer clients to meet your earning needs.

Rate of Growth

Starting out, you'll probably have just a few clients, and you may have to work more than 15 days per month to meet your earnings target. How fast you grow from one to many clients is up to you (and to some degree your market), but many business experts these days advocate soft openings and organic growth — that is, starting and growing at a pace that is manageable and comes without a huge marketing blitz.

Not only is it more economical to save the output of cash on marketing, a soft opening also allows you to refine your delivery of service gradually. Rather than being stressed out or losing business because you have too many clients to give great service, you'll approach that point at a pace that allows you to adjust by hiring help or finding contractors.

In a 2003 business article in *The Waterloo Record*, personal concierge Judy Forwell reported that her first year of business was a "meager existence," but her annual revenue grew within four years to $50,000. The same article reported on another personal concierge who stated that her concierge service, which she ran part time while attending college, generated annual revenues of $30,000. You can read the article online at **www.coldwellbankerpbr.com/media/they%20sweat%20the%20 small%20stuff%20july%2023%2003.pdf**.

"Growth has been slow," admits Bev Riggins of Midwest Concierge Service, who started up in 2004. "A personal concierge service is a new concept in our area, and so it is very slow building it."

She believes that the biggest mistake that "newbies" in the industry make is thinking that they will get rich quickly. "Be realistic," she cautions, but adds encouragingly: "If I can do it in central Illinois, anyone can!"

Number of Clients

How many clients you can manage on your own is a tough figure to nail down, but chances are it's fewer than you'd think. "I think any [number of clients] over 50 would suffer with personal attention falling to the wayside. Remember, many of them would be occasional clients who will only use you when they leave town or things get hectic," advises Jill Burstein, who runs her concierge service in Detroit, MI.

Clients seem to come to you in this business in one of two ways: excruciatingly slowly, and then overwhelmingly. Word of mouth will be your strongest marketing tool, and that's the way that reputation spreads. And although many businesses fail because they fail to plan, businesses are equally susceptible to failure because they don't plan to succeed.

Give some serious thought to how your business will operate: how many days a week you want to work, how many clients you will take on, at what point you'll need some help of your own, etc. Chapter 5 covers hiring assistants or contractors to help you take on more clients and earn more income than a one-person operation can handle.

Although it may seem unnecessary for a small service business, a formal business plan will force you to work these things out. A business plan will be a necessity if you are planning on soliciting outside investors for your concierge business, or if you want to borrow more than $50,000 from a bank or other lender. If you have little experience in business planning, you can use the resources below to assist you.

4.2   Your Business Plan

Your business plan is your map for growth over the next few years. If you start from scratch, you could be launching your business with no clients and no income. If you start part time, you could have a few clients on board before you decide to jump in with both feet. In either case, you are going to want to plan to grow your business to the point where you are earning what you need.

After reading this chapter, and the next one on Running a Personal Concierge Business, you will be able to start creating your own business plan. It is a document you will probably read repeatedly as you start to operate your business. In the meantime, this section will give you an introduction to business planning, walk you through key components of a business plan, and conclude with a variety of resources to help you create your own business plan, including links to further information, business planning software, and free business plan templates.

You'll find sample business plan models you can follow in the resources listed below. If you could use more help with all areas of starting a business, these resources are also excellent sources of additional business start-up information.

Small Business Administration

The SBA offers help with business start-ups and has a variety of programs and services for the small business owner. The site also has links to sample business plans, a business plan workshop, an interactive business planner and more. Visit **http://www.sba.gov/category/navigation-structure/**

starting-managing-business/starting-business/writing-business-plan to find this information. There is at least one SBA office in every state in the United States. Call the Answer Desk at 1-800-U-ASK-SBA (827-5722) or visit their site to find your local SBA office.

SCORE

A non-profit organization, SCORE has over 10,000 volunteers who provide counseling and mentoring to new business start-ups. They also offer an outstanding free business plan template, available in Word or PDF formats, and an online workshop on how to "Develop a Business Plan," as well as many other tips and resources. Visit **www.score.org/resources/business-plans-financial-statements-template-gallery**.

Canada Business Network

You will find a wide range of information at **www.canadabusiness.ca**, including a step-by-step guide to walk you through starting your new business.

Nolo.com

Nolo is a publisher of plain English legal information. Their website also offers free advice on a variety of other small business matters. Go to **www.nolo.com** and click on "Business, LLCs & Corporations."

Business Owner's Toolkit: Small Business Guide

The Business Owner's Toolkit (**www.toolkit.com/small_business_guide**) offers a wide range of advice on a variety of topics of interest to the small business owner.

Entrepreneur: How to Create a Business Plan

Entrepreneur.com explains the seven basic elements of a business plan and lists several resources to help you create one for your business at **http://www.entrepreneur.com/businessplan**.

RBC Royal Bank Business Resources (Canada)

You'll find advice and tips for writing your business plan, as well as several sample business plans. Go to **www.rbcroyalbank.com/sme/index.html**, and click on "Business Plans" under #3 ("Create the Plan").

Business Plan Pro Software

If you want help creating a professional business plan, another option is to buy business planning software from PaloAlto Software (**www.paloalto. com**). The standard version of Business Plan Pro is available for $99.95; the premier version is $159.95. Business Plan Pro offers a step-by-step guide to creating a business plan, as well as 500 samples.

Time Merchants Business Plan

This is a sample business plan for a personal concierge business offering personal errand services. At **www.businessplans.org/Time/Time00. html** you can see the executive summary; scroll to the bottom of the page to find links to other areas of the business plan. This website also offers an explanation of each of the business plan elements under "Guidelines."

Creating a Business Plan

Business planning involves putting on paper all the plans you have for your business. This seems like a tall order, and it is, but once you have completed this step you will feel a tremendous sense of accomplishment. Developing a written business plan helps you maintain your focus with respect to the goals you have for your business and how you will meet them, from the initial stages right through to your exit strategy (your plans to leave the business someday).

In addition, if you are seeking financing for your business from a bank or other lender, they will expect to see a business plan that shows you have a viable business idea with an excellent chance for success. Even if you don't need financing, putting ideas on paper will give you the "road map" of where you want to go with your business and how you are going to get there.

A business plan can also help you avoid costly surprises. If you are considering whether to leave a secure job to start your own business, a business plan can help you determine the resources you will need to start your business and decide when the timing is best for you to get started. While you are working on your business plan, you may start to question some of your previous ideas. You may come up with ideas that are even better or decide to make some changes to ensure you have a greater chance of success.

Many successful business owners have never written a formal, or even informal, business plan. However, having a business plan, even an informal one, in which you set out your business strategy, your mission plan, and lay out the steps you will take to accomplish your goals, can add confidence and credibility to your effort.

While the format of a business plan can vary, one good approach is to divide the body of your business plan into the following sections:

- An executive summary

- Your marketing plan

- Your financial plan

- Your management plan

In addition, your plan should include the following items:

- A cover sheet

- A table of contents

- Mission statement

- Financial projections

- Supporting documents

Executive Summary

Your executive summary is a description of the business you plan to start and operate. Your own company description will be unique to your business. The key for this section is to include information about your business in a way that allows everyone who reads your business plan to understand exactly what your business is all about. They should know after reading the plan that you're on the right path to creating a successful business.

You'll need to state in this section that, as a personal concierge, you'll be operating a service business. Include specifics about the services you'll provide and who you will provide it for. For example, if you will focus on household management, include information about what areas are involved, and point out why your services are important. See the worksheet below to help you in identifying your services.

Your Services

In deciding what kind of concierge services you will offer, consider your life and work experience. If you have retail experience in areas like home supplies or clothing, you might want to market yourself to busy people who need assistance with personal shopping. If you come from a secretarial background, you probably have a lot of insight into this side of the corporate world and could offer your services as an occasional or on-demand personal assistant. Whatever your background, chances are you can apply that somehow to help clients with needs that mesh with your experience. (See Chapter 2 for more information about the many specialties you can choose from.)

Don't pigeon-hole yourself or the services you offer to only things that appeal to you," warns personal concierge Dustyn Shroff. You don't need to assume that you must have a particular niche. Keep in mind that in branching out into various specialties, you shouldn't overlook your primary service: helping your clients. You don't need to assume that you must have a particular niche. However, keep in mind that in branching out into various specialties, you shouldn't overlook your primary service: helping your clients. This could take the form of helping them have a more organized household, having more free time, or feeling confident that pets and home are safe while away on vacation.

You may find the worksheet on the next page helpful for identifying the services you will offer to clients. While you don't need to include the worksheet as part of your business plan, it may help you to focus on the services you will offer and why you chose those.

Other Things to Include

In this section of your business plan you can also discuss the personal concierge industry generally and give details about how your business will operate.

Worksheet for Identifying Services

Describe your planned services in detail. Make sure you are specific (not just "pet sitting," but the exact pet sitting services, like walking, feeding, cleaning cat litter, etc.)

_____

_____

_____

List as many ways you can think of how your services benefit your market. Think about the types of services you'd like to offer, and what experience you already have in that type of service.

_____

_____

_____

List the competitive advantages and disadvantages of your planned services. (Do you already have extensive experience in a particular area? Do you have special education, training, or certification that would make your business rise above the competition? Do you have anything that might hold you back, such as a young family that would prevent you from being available at certain times?)

_____

_____

_____

Describe the market territory you have selected for your business. (Think not only about your immediate community, but also the potential for online customers. Why are your services a good fit for this locality?)

_____

_____

_____

List any potential strategic partners. (Do you have connections with a travel consultant, for example, or a local event planner? Do you know the editor of a local newspaper or magazine who could do a story about your company?)

_____

_____

_____

You can include:

- Statistics reflecting the growth of personal concierge services across the country and in your local area (if any)

- Labor statistics, or other statistics reflecting a need for your services (e.g. Pet sitting services: 63% or 71.1 million U.S. homes have pets, while 57% of all U.S. families are planning a summer vacation away from home; sources: National Pet Owners Survey, 2007; Gallup Poll, May 2006)

- Your legal structure. Will you have a sole proprietorship, for instance, or incorporate? (You can find more about legal structures in section 4.3.4.)

- Your business hours. As a personal concierge, you will most likely need to have flexible hours to accommodate the schedules of your clients, but if you plan only to work from 9 to 5, three days a week, you should make that clear.

- Your business location. Will you work from home or rent an office? Identify the planned location of your business, the type of space you'll have, and why it's conducive to your business.

- Your suppliers. If you will need auxiliary services and products where will you obtain them?

You can also touch on points you will address in other parts of the business plan, such as your marketing plans, your target market (i.e. who your clients will be), and how you will fund your start-up. Conclude the executive summary of your business by clearly identifying your goals and objectives and supporting them with information and knowledge you've acquired about being a personal concierge. It's here that you will explain exactly why you're starting this business and what you hope to accomplish with it.

Your Marketing Plan

Following are key elements of a typical marketing plan. You'll need to do a market analysis to give you (and anyone you might need to show your plan to) a better idea of the potential for your business in your marketplace. You will find additional information to help you plan your marketing strategy in Chapter 6 of this book. Once you've determined how you're going to start marketing your business to which customers, describe it clearly in this section of your business plan.

In addition to a market analysis, you may want to do a SWOT analysis to include in your marketing plan as well. A SWOT analysis is a problem-solving technique that evaluates the Strengths, Weaknesses, Opportunities, and Threats involved in a business venture. It can help you determine if your objectives are achievable and, if so, what factors may help or hinder your company's achievement of those objectives.

Strengths and weaknesses are internal to your company, while opportunities and threats are external to the business. Strengths and opportunities can help you achieve your objectives, while weaknesses and threats can get in the way of success. With respect to your personal concierge business, your strengths might lie in the types of services you can offer, services that might not be offered by another, similar business in your market. A weakness might be that your car is not reliable. An opportunity might be present in a trend that you have identified that no one else has yet exploited. Threats from the outside might include a variety of things, such as economic declines, a local industry downturn, or direct competitors.

Identifying possible threats and opportunities is essential to creating an effective marketing plan. You don't want to start offering services that nobody wants or that others are already filling a need for. You should begin by identifying your competition, your potential clients, and any risks associated with your business start-up; for example, any potential for high business (or personal) liability.

Clients

The most important elements of a good marketing plan are defining your market and knowing your clients. Knowing your clients is important because it allows you to tailor your services to accommodate them.

You don't want to limit yourself to a market that is too narrow — that can limit the scope of your business once it's underway. For example, if you want to specialize in pet sitting, you'll have many more prospective clients if you target "dog and cat owners" rather than "dog owners." And targeting all "pet owners" will give you an even larger market.

Quantify your potential client base and use your marketing plan to highlight the ready market that eagerly awaits your services.

Competition

Businesses – yours included – compete for customers, market share, publicity and so forth. It's smart to know who your competitors are and exactly what they're doing. In order to provide services that are different or better, you need to look carefully at your competitors' products and services, how they're promoting them, and who's buying them.

Here are some ways you can identify some of your competitors:

- Search online for your specialty and location using a search engine like Google to see what comes up

- Look through online directories such as the Yellow Pages

- Check with your local Chamber of Commerce to find similar businesses

- Check listings on association websites

- Check for competitors' ads in local newspapers

You can also do a competition analysis after you find out who your main competitors are. Start by listing your top five competitors and then list the services they offer and any special strengths and/or weaknesses of their businesses.

Target Markets

Discovering who your potential clients are will help you to create your business to address their needs. For example, if you would like to open a business that caters to young urban professionals but live in an area where 75% of the population is over 65, you may find yourself struggling. On the other hand, if you want to sell your services to those seniors, you need to discover what types of services you can offer that will appeal to them.

You may choose to market only to individual clients or you may decide to include corporate clients in your target market. You might also choose to market exclusively to corporate clients. This choice is yours and will depend mainly on your own experience and the types of services you will offer.

Here are a few examples of the types of clients you could target in each category:

Individual

- Wealthy people
- Seniors
- Busy professionals
- Career mothers
- People with large families
- Disabled people
- New home buyers
- Pet owners
- People purchasing or selling a home
- Men (e.g. gift-purchasing services)

Corporate

- Small companies who don't need full-time assistance
- Companies needing occasional event planning services
- Companies needing some office organization
- Companies needing assistance with travel planning
- Executives (gift buying, part-time personal assistance, etc.)
- Apartment complexes
- Smaller hotels
- Gated communities

No matter what type of client you choose to target, be sure to provide details and supporting data in your marketing plan that explains why you have chosen those types of clients.

Pricing

You'll learn more about setting your fees later in this guide in section 5.2, but for now be aware that you should address this subject, at least briefly, in your business plan. This section should consider factors such as competitive pricing, costs of labor and materials, overhead and so forth. After you've read section 5.2, you'll have a better idea of what to include in this section of your business plan.

Marketing Strategy

You'll need to think about how you'll advertise and promote your business. Have a budget in mind, or at least set percentages of your business income that you'll invest back into marketing the business. Include a detailed description of your marketing strategy in this section of your business plan.

Your Financial Plan

Since financial management is so crucial to running a successful business, your business plan should describe projected revenues, your start-up costs and your ongoing operating costs. The start-up budget includes all the costs necessary to get your business up and running. Operating costs are ongoing expenses, such as advertising, utilities, rent and so forth.

You'll also want to include cash flow forecasts, both monthly and annually, to highlight your projected revenues and expenses. This will help you to estimate more accurately your expenses and know how much you will need to earn in order to pay your bills. This is an essential part of planning your ongoing budgets.

In addition, include a short description of your accounting and bookkeeping systems. If you plan to hire an accounting or bookkeeping firm, state that here. If you will do your own bookkeeping using an accounting software program such as QuickBooks, then state that, too.

Be sure to include the following financial information in this section of your business plan:

Start-up Budget

Include legal and professional fees, licenses and permits, equipment, supplies, stationery, marketing expenses. (More information about start-up budgets is provided in section 4.1.) Include a short discussion of your financial situation at start-up and what you plan to do with the money you (and/or your investors) are putting into the company at the outset.

Operating Budget

Make a budget for your first three to six months of operation, including expenses such as: personnel (even if it's only your own salary), insurance, rent, marketing expenses (marketing materials, advertising, etc.), legal and accounting fees, supplies, utilities, printing, membership dues, subscriptions, and taxes.

Financial Statements

Financial statements you include here will be for the most part projections of your future yearly accounting cycles. You should include cash flow projections, first year projected income statement, and a balance sheet (statement of assets vs. liabilities) at start-up. Include cash flow projections for at least the next five years.

Exit Strategy

It may seem a little premature to being thinking about how you will leave your business, but most good business people have some idea of how they will eventually wind down their companies. Having an exit strategy clarifies what you would like to see happen with your company someday in the future when you no longer wish to run it.

For example, you may hope to expand your business so that it becomes large enough for some large corporation to take it over or to turn it into a franchise operation. Or maybe you want to retire at age 55 and turn it over to your niece, who will need to be trained in all the aspects of running your company before you retire. Whatever the ultimate fate of your company you should include a brief statement of how someday you will wind down your involvement in it.

Your Management Plan

No matter how large your business is, managing it requires organization and leadership. Your management plan will therefore address issues such as:

- Your background and business experience and how they'll benefit your concierge business

- The members of your management team (even if you'll be the only member)

- Assistance you expect to receive (this can be financial help, mentoring, business coaching, professional advice, or other forms of aid)

- The duties for which you and any employees will be responsible

- Plans for hiring employees, contractors, and industry partners (like limo services, travel consultants, event planners or anyone else who will provide you with auxiliary services for clients) either now or in the future

- A general overview of how your business will be run

The Extras

In addition to these major areas, your business plan should include the extras mentioned below. You can find more information about these extras in the resources mentioned at the beginning of this section of the guide.

A Cover Sheet

This identifies your business and explains the purpose of the business plan. Be sure to include your name, the name of the business and the name of any partners, if applicable; your address, phone number, e-mail address and other pertinent information.

Table of Contents

This goes just under your cover sheet and tells what's included in your business plan. Use major headings and subheadings to identify the contents. The best time to do the table of contents is after you have completed everything else in your business plan, using it as your guide.

Financial Projections

This is an estimate of how much money you'll need to start your business, and how much you expect to earn. If you're familiar with spreadsheet programs like Microsoft Excel, you can include graphs. Remember to support your projections with explanations.

Supporting Documents

If you will be seeking start-up funding, you'll be expected to include financial information. This may include your personal (and business, if applicable) tax returns for the past three years, a copy of a lease agreement if you will rent office space, or any other documents a potential lender might want to see.

4.3 Legal Matters

Running any small business, even a unique and fun one like a personal concierge service, requires that you pay attention to money matters, and stay on the right side of the law. Here are some strategies for you to learn and use, and a number of resources for further study.

4.3.1 Choosing a Name

The name that you choose for your business says a lot about the way you want your business to be perceived. For this reason, you should invest some time and thought into selecting the right one.

Options to Choose From

Many personal concierges choose to use their own names as part of the business name, such as *Janie's Concierge Service*, or *Errands by Janie*.

The perception is that Janie is the person clients will be dealing with, and that Janie will stand behind her work. It implies that the client will have personal contact with Janie, and that the business is small and personal.

If you choose to go with a different name for your business than your own, there are several considerations. Your name should tell clients a bit about what you do, so consider using the words "errands," "concierge," or "assistant." As an example, a name like "More Time 4 U" doesn't tell the client that you are not a watch repair shop or child-minding service.

> **TIP:** Services are often listed alphabetically. If you choose a name that starts with a letter close to the beginning of the alphabet, you'll be listed closer to the top of service directories. Not to say that you need to call yourself "AAA Concierge," but every little thing helps!

No matter what you name your business, be forewarned that some people are going to be confused about what you do. Personal concierge service is a fledgling industry, and many people are simply unfamiliar with the concept. Concierges are generally associated with hotels, and it doesn't help that people offering the same services call themselves assistants, helpers, Girl or Guy Fridays, and even lifestyle managers. Have a 30-second speech you can use to explain succinctly what you do — you can use or modify the one provided for you in section 6.5.1.

If you are planning to specialize in a certain type of service or client, you can hint at that in the name of your business. Just be aware that names can be limiting as well. For example, if you call yourself "Senior Saver" and then find out that seniors don't generate enough business, you're looking at reprinting a lot of business cards and brochures. Similarly, a name that includes your town or city won't travel with you if you move, or allow you to open offices in other cities when you become a raging success.

Time is an odd thing to sell in a way, since its value is unique to the individual. When you sell your concierge services, you are also selling family bonding, reduced stress, and peace of mind. Therefore, a name that conjures up the "emotional value" of what you do is also appropriate. Keep this tip in mind when you design your marketing materials too.

Legal Issues

It goes without saying that the name of your business must not infringe on the copyright of competing businesses. If you've thought of something catchy, start with an informal Internet or Yellow Pages search to eliminate some names right away. In the U.S., the place to start a more formal search is with the U.S. Patent and Trademark Office. You can conduct a free search of the database at **www.uspto.gov/trademarks/ index.jsp**.

In Canada, the database for name searches is the government's Newly Upgraded Automated Name Search (NUANS). There is a $20 charge (plus tax) for each search. Visit **www.nuans.com** for more information about using this service.

If you are doing business using a business name other than your full name, then you will have to file a "Doing Business As" fictitious name, or DBA, in many jurisdictions. A DBA name registration is required if you are using any fictitious name to do business. For example, if your name is Joe Smith you can use Joe Smith Personal Concierge Services without filing a DBA. But if you decide to call your business Joe's Personal Concierge Services or Smith Personal Concierge Services, you would need to register either of those names. Similarly, any other name that is not your own full name would need to be registered.

Formal registration of your fictitious business name allows you to conduct all aspects of your business, such as accepting payments, advertising and any other activities such as banking you undertake for your business. Check with your local municipality for their requirements with respect to a DBA name registration.

Registering your business name is not a necessity for unincorporated small businesses, but it will prevent others from using your name. The link to Nolo.com on the next page will connect you with more information about the legalities of choosing a business name. A good place to find more information about naming your business in Canada is the Corporations Canada website, which features a brochure on the subject.

- *Nolo*
  www.nolo.com/legal-encyclopedia/business-name

- *Corporations Canada: Choosing a Name*
  http://strategis.gc.ca/epic/site/cd-dgc.nsf/en/cs01191e.html

4.3.2   Insurance

Without a doubt, your personal concierge business will need insurance. When you accept money from a client for concierge services, they will hold you responsible for any perceived negligence on your part. In addition, you will need to protect the assets of your company against other potential disasters like theft, fire, and other forms of damage. You may want to consider some of the other types of insurance coverage listed in this section as well.

You can also check out the National Association for the Self-Employed (**www.nase.org**), which offers reasonably priced insurance for self-employed people. Hiscox Insurance has a program available specifically for home-based businesses that you can learn more about online at **www.hiscoxusa.com/small-business-insurance/home-based-business-insurance**.

Insurers and Costs

While finding insurance coverage probably won't be a problem, your insurance agent might have trouble classifying your business. This is important because different risk classifications have different costs, so you'll need to be sure you're in a category that will leave you paying less if possible.

Jill Burstein, who runs her business in Detroit, says, "Most insurance folks don't have a clue as to how to classify you, so they will try to put you in the janitorial, interior design, or consulting groups, among others. We all talk to our insurance professionals and we all get different answers. Whatever they tell you, get it in writing!" she advises.

You may need to consult with more than one insurance company to get a decent quote. Personal concierge services are a relatively new concept, and as such, insurance companies are not sure exactly where to place them on the list of risky business. To save you some leg work, sit down with a broker and explain to them exactly what services you plan to offer. Then let them shop you around to their contacts.

As one personal concierge business owner explained to us, there are a few insurers who have policies designed specifically for those running personal concierge businesses:

> *"There are still challenges in acquiring business insurance for the personal concierge industry; however, strides are being made to lessen that. I found two independent insurance brokers who were able to provide me with quotes on policies that have been established for the Concierge and Errand Services category. The cost of insurance, as I've seen, can range from $500 to $2,000 per year."*
>
> — Delmar Johnson,
> The Concierge Place,
> Raleigh, NC

"I know of one insurance company (Burlington) that has a category for personal concierges. They're a well-kept industry secret," says Jill Burstein, She adds, "I pay about $1,500 dollars annually to insure. Pet sitting was a separate insurance, but less than $200. It depends on what you do."

If you would like to contact the Burlington Insurance Group to enquire about this program, visit their website at **www.burlingtoninsurance. com/BIG-Overview.aspx** for more information.

Liability Insurance

To protect yourself and your assets in the case of a lawsuit, you will need to obtain professional liability insurance. Often this type of insurance can be fairly inexpensive. "For a general liability policy with no driving of clients, I pay around $400 per year," says personal concierge Bev Riggins, who is located in central Illinois.

One type of liability insurance, known as Errors and Omissions Insurance, protects you against loss if you are sued for alleged negligence. It could pay judgments against you (up to the limits of the policy) along with any legal fees you incur defending yourself.

Certain services that carry more liability risk, such as childcare and driving your clients around, will increase your rates. Consider whether or not the potential income from these services is worth it. "Vehicle insurance should have a rider on top of your regular auto insurance to cover any valuables you might transport for a client," adds Jill Burstein.

Property and Equipment Insurance

This insurance covers losses to your personal property from damage or theft. If your business will be located in your home, you might be covered by your homeowner's insurance, but be sure to check with your insurance provider to see if this is the case.

If you plan on working out of your home, inquire with your insurance provider about an equipment add-on to your homeowner's policy. You'll need property insurance only on the equipment you have in your office (i.e. the contents); the owner of the building you rent space in normally would pay for insurance on the property itself.

Depending on your location, you may also need flood, hurricane or other natural disaster insurance. In the event that your property or equipment is damaged or destroyed, business interruption insurance covers ongoing expenses until you're up and running again. These policies may also have provisions for loaned equipment until permanent replacements can be obtained.

Life and Disability Insurance

If you become sick for an extended period or otherwise disabled, your business could be in jeopardy. Disability insurance would provide a portion of your income while you're not able to work. If you're not covered by a spouse's health insurance you should look into that as well. You can compare health insurance quotes across the U.S. at **www. ehealthinsurance.com**.

If your family will depend on you for earning the only income, then you should also purchase life insurance. That way, if anything happens to you, your family is protected.

Workers' Compensation Insurance

Most states and all provinces require that small business owners who hire others carry workers' compensation insurance. For more about these obligations in the U.S., visit the Office of Workers' Compensation Programs website at **www.dol.gov/owcp**. The link for state by state information about employer obligations is "State Workers' Compensation Laws." In Canada, visit the Association of Workers' Compensation Boards of Canada at **www.awcbc.org** (click on the "Employer Resources" link) for more information.

Business Interruption Insurance

This insurance covers your bills and lost profit while you are out of operation for a covered loss, such as a fire. Remember that even if your business is shut down the bills will keep coming. This type of insurance covers ongoing expenses like rent or taxes until your business is up and running again.

Bonding

Bonding is basically like insurance. A company bonds its employees if there is any risk of illegal or fraudulent activity on the part of those employees. If an employee acts dishonestly and the company loses money as a result, bonding helps to protect against these losses.

Bonding is generally not necessary until you actually plan to hire employees, in which case it will protect you from liability for their actions (e.g., theft from your clients). If you do take on employees now or in the future, ask your insurance professional to evaluate the pros and cons of fidelity bonding for your business.

4.3.3 Registration and Taxes

To obtain a local business license, you'll need to fill out some forms and pay an annual fee. Contact your town, city, or county office for more information, or check out the information on business licenses at the Small Business Administration's website mentioned earlier in this section.

All U.S. businesses that have employees need an employer identification number (EIN) with which to report employee tax withholding, unemployment and worker's compensation information. In Canada this is the T-4. Also in Canada, you must charge your clients GST (Goods and Services Tax) if you earn more than $30,000 in four consecutive quarters.

If you plan to purchase wholesale items for your clients (e.g., organizing products) and sell them at a mark-up, you'll need to register to collect sales tax and submit it to the government. If you are self-employed, you'll pay a self-employment tax to contribute to your Social Security.

Note that you may need to acquire business registrations before banks, suppliers and vendors will do business with you. Contact the Internal Revenue Service or Revenue Canada office in your area for more information. As a self-employed business person, you will also want to consult a good accountant or tax lawyer to advise you on your tax situation.

- *Nolo.com Small Business Resources: Licenses and Permits*
  www.nolo.com/legal-encyclopedia/business-permits

- *Internal Revenue Service: Small Business/Self-Employed*
  www.irs.gov/businesses/small/index.html

- *Canada Revenue Agency*
  www.cra-arc.gc.ca/tx/bsnss/tpcs/gst-tps/menu-eng.html

- *Canada Tax Information: Province by Province*
  www.cra-arc.gc.ca/tx/bsnss/prv_lnks-eng.html

4.3.4   Your Business Legal Structure

Like all entrepreneurs, you will be faced with the decision of how to legally structure your business operation. Your business structure affects your taxes and your liability (i.e. your responsibility) for any debts of the business. Which structure you choose will also have an impact on how much it costs to start and run your business. The sole proprietorship is the least costly way to go into business, but it doesn't afford some of the legal protections of a corporate structure.

Basically, there are four forms of ownership: sole proprietorships, partnerships, LLCs, and corporations. What makes sense for you depends on the type of business you have in mind. In this section we will look at the advantages and disadvantages of each for businesses, including the characteristics and benefits of the various types.

Sole Proprietorship

A sole proprietorship is any business operated by one single individual without any formal structure or registration requirements. A sole proprietorship is the simplest and least expensive business legal structure when you are starting out. It is also the easiest because it requires less paperwork and you can report your business income on your personal tax return. One drawback to this type of business is that you are personally liable for any debts of the business.

In other words, without going through any formal processes, you can begin your concierge business simply by getting the word out that you're in business. However, there are usually business licenses and permits required by local municipalities in order for you to conduct business. The costs of these licenses are usually minimal, but be sure to check with your local municipal licensing office.

Here are some of the advantages and disadvantages of starting your business under the sole proprietorship model:

Advantages

- Easy to start
- Low start-up costs
- Flexible and informal
- Business losses can often be deducted from personal income for tax purposes

Disadvantages

- Unlimited personal liability: the sole proprietor can be held personally responsible for debts and judgments placed against the business, including losses resulting from any dishonest actions by employees. This means that all personal income and assets (your house, your car, your furniture, etc.), not just those of the business, can be seized to recoup losses or pay damages.

- All business income earned must be reported and is taxed as personal income.

- More difficult to raise capital for the business

Partnerships

Another business structure that some small business owners choose over sole proprietorship is the partnership. A partnership is, precisely as its name implies, a business venture entered into by two or more people with the intent to carry on business and earn profits together. Partnerships can be beneficial because the workload and finances can be shared, and partners with differing areas of expertise can increase business opportunities.

You must register your partnership with a corporate registry. This does not mean that you must incorporate, only that you are making a formal declaration of entering into business with another person or persons. Be sure to consult your local business registry and a lawyer specializing in business registry. The primary purpose for doing this is for each partner to protect himself or herself concerning issues such as sharing profits, liability and dissolving the partnership equitably.

Below are some of the advantages and disadvantages to partnerships:

Advantages

- More initial equity for start-up costs

- Broader areas of expertise can lead to increased opportunities

- Lower start-up costs than incorporation

- Some tax advantages

Disadvantages

- All partners are equally liable for the other's mistakes with the same liability as a sole proprietorship

- Profits and losses must be shared

- The business must be dissolved and reorganized when a partner leaves

Working With a Partner

A good partnership requires a bit of planning if it is to run smoothly. You may want to have an attorney set up a legal partnership, spelling out what each partner contributes to and takes out of the business.

Beyond any legal issues, before going into business with a partner you should spend many hours talking about how you will work together, including:

- what each of you will be responsible for

- how you will make decisions on a day-to-day basis

- what percentage of the business each of you will own

- how you see the business developing in the future

- what you expect from each other

During your discussions you can learn if there are any areas where you need to compromise. You can avoid future misunderstandings by putting the points you have agreed on into a written "partnership agreement" that covers any possibility you can think of (including one of you leaving the business in the future).

Incorporation

Chances are, you won't be starting out by incorporating your business. For most entrepreneurs just starting out in business, the costs and the paperwork involved are simply too overwhelming. However, as your company grows and you take on more work and start to hire employees, you may want to consider incorporating for the various legal protections and tax advantages this form of business structure offers.

Incorporation of a business means that a separate, legal corporate entity has been created for the purpose of conducting business. Like an individual, corporations can be taxed, sued, can enter contractual agreements and are liable for their debts. Corporations are characterized by shareholders, a board of directors and various company officers. As such, ownership interests can be freely transferred.

Creating a corporation requires filing of numerous documents to legalize your business, as well as formally naming a president, shareholders, and director(s), all of whom can be a single person as set out in the company charter. As the rules and forms required for incorporation vary from state to state and province to province, it's best to consult your local business licensing office or a local lawyer specializing in incorporation.

While it is probably best to seek legal expertise when incorporating, if you have the expertise and knowledge, you can incorporate your own business or use one of the many online resources that specialize in these matters. Here are a few websites offering such services, often for only a couple of hundred dollars:

- *BizFilings*
  www.bizfilings.com

- *The Company Corporation*
  www.incorporate.com

- *Intuit—My Corporation.com*
  www.mycorporation.com

- *Form-a-Corp, Inc.*
  www.form-a-corp.com

Here is a list of some of the advantages and disadvantages to incorporating your consulting firm.

Advantages

- Protect personal assets and income from liability by separating your business income and assets from your personal.

- Corporations get greater tax breaks and incentives

- Ownership can be sold or transferred if the owner wishes to retire or leave the business

- Banks and other lending institutions tend to have more faith in incorporated businesses so raising capital is easier

Disadvantages

- Increased start-up costs

- Substantial increase in paperwork

- Your business losses cannot be offset against your personal income

- Corporations are more closely regulated

An S Corporation is similar to the corporation in most ways, but with some tax advantages. The corporation can pass its earnings and profits on as dividends to the shareholder(s). However, as an employee of the corporation you do have to pay yourself a wage that meets the government's reasonable standards of compensation just as if you were paying someone else to do your job.

Limited Liability Company

A Limited Liability Company is a newer type of business legal structure in the U.S. It is a combination of a sole proprietorship (where there is only one member of the LLC) or partnership and a corporation, and is considered to have some of the best attributes of each, including limited personal liability.

An LLC business structure gives you the benefits of a partnership or S corporation while providing personal asset protection like a corporation. Similar to incorporating, there will be substantial paperwork involved in establishing this business structure. LLCs have flexible tax options, but are usually taxed like a partnership.

Here are some of the advantages and disadvantages of LLCs:

Advantages

- Limited liability similar to a corporation

- Tax advantages similar to a corporation

- Can be started with one (except in Massachusetts) or more members like a sole proprietorship or partnership

Disadvantages

- More costly to start than a sole proprietorship or partnership

- Consensus among members may become an issue

- LLC dissolves if any member leaves

In the end, choosing a business legal structure for your company is a personal choice, and the advantages and disadvantages should be considered thoroughly. Many new business owners begin their independent venture as a sole proprietorship because of the low costs, and incorporate as the business grows and the business become larger and more complex.

For more on business structures take a look at the resources available at FindLaw.com or the excellent advice offered at the Quicken website. For some additional government resources to help you decide which structure to choose, try the Small Business Administration in the U.S. and Canada Business Services for Entrepreneurs in Canada.

- *FindLaw*
  http://smallbusiness.findlaw.com/ incorporation-and-legal-structures

- *U.S. Small Business Administration*
  Click on "Starting & Managing a Business", then on "Establishing a Business", then on "Incorporating & Registering Your Business"
  www.sba.gov

- *Canada Business Services for Entrepreneurs*
  www.canadabusiness.ca/eng/125/141

4.4   Financial Matters

4.4.1   Keeping Track of Your Finances

Being self-employed offers you the freedom to set your own schedule, work from home and choose your clients. However, this also means that you will be responsible for keeping track of your earnings and any applicable deductions. The only way to really know where your business stands is by having adequate financial records at your fingertips.

Keep accurate track of all invoices, receipts, telephone bills (related to your business), and other business paperwork. If you're not used to keeping receipts for everything you buy, you should quickly develop this habit. Any supplies you buy for your office, right down to pens and paperclips, are legitimate business expenses and deductible at tax time. You don't have to print hard copies of everything, but be certain that the information is easily accessible if you need to look up or produce something.

Knowing exactly where your money is going will help you plan better and cut back on any unnecessary expenses. So, again, make it a habit to ask for a receipt for every expense related to business. At a glance, you should be able to see how much money has been brought in, how much money has been paid out, what amounts are waiting to be collected, and what debt amounts are still owed.

Bookkeeping System

Your bookkeeping system is a record of your expenses and revenues. Monitoring your expenses and revenues with a consistent bookkeeping system will help you build a more profitable company. By making this part of your daily activities, your financial position will be much clearer, and you will have the records you will need at tax time.

The first step is to choose an accounting method for your business. The two basic types are the accrual accounting method and the single-entry cash accounting method. The accrual method is not generally used in service businesses because it categorizes money that is still owed as collected money, even if you haven't received payment yet.

The single-entry cash method is much simpler, since all incoming money is posted as a credit and any money spent is posted as a debit. Your credits minus your debits will equal your ledger balance.

A good way to learn more about using a bookkeeping system is to take a small business accounting course, as mentioned earlier. These usually are fairly inexpensive, last a few weeks or a few months, and many are offered online. Check with your local college educational extension or continuing education departments to find out more, or check online at **www.petersons.com** or **www.schoolfinder.com**.

Bookkeeping Software

When in doubt, get some help with your bookkeeping efforts. One solution is to invest in accounting computer software such as Intuit's Quicken or QuickBooks (**www.intuit.com**) or Sage 50 (**http://na.sage.com/Sage-50-Accounting-US**). You can buy the basic edition from either company for less than $300.

These powerful, bundled software packages can help you manage the following accounting functions:

- Accounts payable

- Accounts receivable and collections

- General ledger, balance sheet, and cash flow

- Invoicing and billing

- Payroll

- Report generation

- Stock and inventory

- Tax deductible expense tracking

In addition to these functions, a program like QuickBooks lets you import all of your financial data into its QuickTax program, to make your tax filing simple and painless.

4.4.2   Financial Reports

There are several key financial reports that you will want to regularly update and maintain as a small business owner:

- Cash flow statement

- Balance sheet

- Income statement

Cash Flow Statement

This is a basic record of income and expenses, otherwise known as credits and debits. It is usually tracked on a daily or weekly basis and then tallied up for a given month. When you look at this data across several months, you can perform cash flow projections for upcoming months. Knowing your cash flow will tell you if there is enough money to pay the bills.

Generally, you will create two kinds of cash flow statements, one on a monthly basis to keep track of cash in and cash out for each month, and a second one on an annual basis. Below you will find a sample monthly cash flow statement. Notice that it includes revenue streams from a variety of services. You can adapt this to whatever services you choose to offer and however you choose to classify your revenues.

As mentioned in section 4.2, cash flow projections are an essential part of your business plan. You can use the example on the next page to create monthly cash flow statements and, by using the totals in each category for each month, an annual total cash flow statement.

Balance Sheet

This helpful document compares your total assets to your total liabilities. Assets include current assets like cash, prepaid expenses, accounts receivable, and long term assets like property and equipment owned by your business (you wouldn't include your house or car or anything else you personally own). Liabilities consist of any owed amounts such

Sample Cash Flow Worksheet

MONTH:	JANUARY
CASH RECEIPTS	
Pet sitting services	
Personal organizing	
Household management	
Personal shopping	
TOTAL	
CASH DISBURSEMENTS	
Start-up costs	
Advertising	
Bank charges	
Fees & dues	
Insurance	
Loans-Principal	
Loans-Interest	
Licenses & taxes	
Purchases for resale	
Office supplies	
Professional fees	
Rent	
Telephone	
Internet	
Utilities	
Wages & benefits	
Owner's draw	
MONTHLY SURPLUS OR DEFICIT (Cash less Disbursements)	
TO DATE SURPLUS OR DEFICIT*	

Monthly surplus to date is calculated by carrying through any deficit or surplus from month to month.

Sample Balance Sheet

[Company Name]
for *[e.g. 12-month]* period ending *[Month, Day]*, 20__

ASSETS	
Accounts receivable	$
Cash in bank	$
Cash on hand	$
Furniture/equipment	$
Petty cash	$
(less depreciation)	$
TOTAL ASSETS	$

LIABILITIES	
Accounts payable	$
Loan payments	$
Leases/rentals	$
Taxes	$
TOTAL LIABILITIES	$

EQUITY	
Less owner's salary	$
Net profit	$
Working capital	$
TOTAL EQUITY	$
TOTAL EQUITY AND LIABILITIES	$

as loans, taxes, and accounts payable. By subtracting the liabilities from the assets, you will discover your owner's equity amount.

Balance sheets are usually prepared on a quarterly, semi-yearly, or annual basis. And, since a balance sheet is essentially a snapshot of what your business owns and owes at a particular point in time, it's a good idea to include a balance sheet as part of your business plan's financial plan section. This way, anyone who looks at your business plan can see at a glance your financial position at start-up.

A sample balance sheet is included on the previous page.

Income Statement

This report is also called a profit and loss statement, or P & L. It shows all generated income minus the business expenses, resulting in the gross profit before taxes. Like a balance sheet, this document you only need to create this once every 3, 6, or 12 months. With an income statement you can see at a glance where you stand at tax time.

A sample income statement is included on the next page.

4.4.3   Other Financial Considerations

Financial Experts

Just as people will hire you as an expert to help them solve some of their personal and business problems, you may want to hire experts to assist with your finances. An accountant or tax advisor can be expensive (e.g. you might pay $100 per hour compared to the $20 per hour you might pay a bookkeeper), but their advice could possibly save you hundreds or even thousands of dollars at tax time.

An accountant is someone who takes all your recorded transactions and creates financial reports, such as those mentioned earlier, in order to analyze your business. They can also provide valuable financial guidance and help with filing tax returns. To lower your expenses when hiring an accountant try to do some basic bookkeeping so the professional accountant doesn't have to sort through and organize your paperwork. Remember, they charge by the hour.

Sample Income Statement

Income Statement *[Company Name]*

for *[e.g. 12-month]* period ending *[Month, Day]*, 20__

REVENUE ($)

Pet sitting...$_____
Personal organizing...$_____
Household management..$_____
Personal shopping ....$_____
Total Sales...$_____

COST OF GOODS SOLD

Inventory and material purchases..............................$_____
Transportation...$_____
Supplies...$_____
Total Cost of Goods Sold.......................................$_____

Gross Profit..$_____

EXPENSES

Lease ....$_____
Insurance..$_____
Licences ....$_____
Office supplies...$_____
Utilities ....$_____
Wages..$_____
Telephone & internet...$_____
Vehicle expense ....$_____
Interest..$_____
Depreciation ....$_____
Repairs & maintenance ....$_____
Total Expenses ....$_____

Total Earnings Before Taxes..................................$_____
Taxes ....$_____

Net Income for the Month.....................................$_____

If you find yourself so busy with providing concierge services that you don't have time to do your own bookkeeping, consider hiring a part-time bookkeeper on a contract basis to do your bookkeeping for you. A bookkeeper can assist with your daily and weekly transactions with respect to accounts payable and accounts receivable. They will record all of your incoming money and process any money that you owe.

Depending on how busy you are, it may take the bookkeeper a few hours per week to get your books up to date and balance them with your bank statements.

You can find a bookkeeper by checking your local newspaper classified ads or in the Yellow Pages under "Bookkeeping Service."

Financial Institution

Open a business account at a bank, trust company or credit union, even if you are using only your own name to do business. And use this only for paying the bills of the company and your own salary, which you then deposit in your personal account.

You can shop around to find a financial institution that is supportive of small business, or use the same one that you use for your personal banking. In addition to your checking account, a financial institution may provide you with a corporate credit card you can use to make purchases for your business, and a merchant credit card account if you want to accept credit card payments from your customers.

Get a style of business check that makes it impossible for you not to record checks you've written. Avoid using electronic payments unless you can print out a receipt for them. You want to create a paper trail for your business account so you are able to:

- Prove your deductible expenses at tax time

- Create a balance sheet that lenders may request from time to time

- See at a glance where your money has gone

4.5 Your Office

4.5.1 Office Location

The first thing you will need for your new business is a place to work. Wherever you choose to work, whether at home or in rented location, you will need office space in which to take care of the daily tasks of running your business. These tasks can include answering telephone calls and emails, bookkeeping, scheduling, etc. So you will need a space that can allow you privacy and enough room to equip an office with all the essentials needed to effectively run your business.

Working From Home

A spare bedroom or space in the basement can be easily converted into a functional, even attractive office.

Wherever you choose to set up your home office, be sure that it is a space that is off limits to your family, since client confidentiality is essential. In addition to this, you want a quiet space where you can answer client calls and do your paperwork without interruptions from family. Also, having a spot that is set aside from your living areas in this way will allow you to close the door at the end of your workday and walk away from the office.

There are a few tax breaks you can take advantage of if you have a home office, too. You can deduct from your income taxes a percent of your mortgage payment and property taxes (or rent) and a share of utilities and maintenance costs. There are various methods to make those calculations, but by far the easiest – and most acceptable to the tax authorities in both the U.S. and Canada is to use an entire room for your office and use it for no other purpose.

In the U.S., IRS Publication 587 has information on how to compute the calculation and file the deduction. You can download this information by visiting the IRS website and searching for the publication numbers from the search engine on the front page. The Canada Revenue Agency has similar online services. (See section 4.3.3 earlier in this chapter for more about your business tax obligations and links to the IRS and Canada Revenue Agency.)

Renting Space

While a home office works well for most personal concierges, others prefer to rent a separate space. A separate space can create a better impression if you plan to have clients visit you. Some of the larger personal concierge companies have offices, particularly those who have hired employees. Others just feel more professional if they have somewhere other than a designated room in their house to go every day.

Office Space

Remember that you don't absolutely have to rent office space to run a business like a professional. One of the main reasons people come into this industry is to give themselves more freedom and flexibility, and spending several hundred dollars a month for office rental, plus additional time and travel expenses, may be defeating the purpose.

If you do decide to rent office space, try to secure a short-term lease— six months or even month to month. Don't get locked into a one or two-year lease before your business is firmly established. Also, you might consider renting office furniture and computer equipment rather than purchasing outright.

Look for a place that is convenient to get to from your home, and that gives you quick access to any services you may need, such as your bank or even a good restaurant or coffee shop. Pick an area that suits your needs and fits your budget. For more advice on what to consider before renting space visit **www.nolo.com/legal-encyclopedia/commercial-lease**.

Serviced Offices

Another option for renting office space, particularly if you plan to market to corporate clients and meet with them there, is to find a professional, serviced office where several professionals share a common receptionist and other office facilities such as conference rooms, printers, copiers, and so on. Many of these types of office rentals also offer additional administrative services like typing, correspondence, filing, etc. This can be an economical option for setting up a professional space for your business. Prices vary but can start as low as $500 per month depending on your location and any extra services offered.

There are many websites where you can find these services. One example is Instant Offices (**www.instant-offices.com**), which is a searchable directory of serviced office space available all across North America and the world. You can also type "serviced offices" and the name of your city into your favorite search engine or look in the Yellow Pages under "Office Rentals" to find more.

4.5.2 Office Equipment and Supplies

You will need a variety of office equipment and supplies for your concierge business. If you don't already have everything you need, you will have initial expenses for these items. However, once your office is stocked, your ongoing expenses should be minimal.

Office Supply List

Of course you will need the basic supplies any business needs, including pens and pencils, paper, stapler, clips, Post-Its, scissors, tape, Liquid Paper, etc. By looking around your home, you can probably gather together most of the basic office supplies needed to set up your new company headquarters. However, if you are starting a home office from scratch, you'll need to visit your local discount office supply store.

Check with local office supply stores like Staples and Office Depot to find out about sales on supplies and on any of the larger items listed below. The sales reps who work there can also be of assistance when it comes to getting help putting together everything you need for your office.

The major furniture requirements will be a desk or large table, a desk chair, a filing cabinet or file box, and shelves for the storage of reference materials. Useful office supplies to have close at hand include these practical items:

- Business card file
- Calculator
- Correction fluid or tape
- CD ROMs/flash drive for backing up computer files
- Day planner or PDA
- Envelopes, #10 size and 9" x 12" (business size)
- File folders, file labels, file jackets, and expanding file pockets
- Glue stick
- Paper clips and binder clips
- Pens, pencils, colored pencils, and markers
- Printer paper and stationery
- Stamps and return address labels
- Stapler and box of staples
- Tape with dispenser
- Writing pads and self-stick note pads

Any of the stores listed below can help you stock your home office with supplies. Most items can be ordered online, too.

- *OfficeMax*
  www.officemax.com

- *Office Depot*
  www.officedepot.com

- *Staples*
  www.staples.com

Computer and Software

Most people these days have access to a computer. However, if you don't have your own computer, you should consider buying or leasing one for your business as soon as you can afford it. In addition to the computer, it's a good idea to get a printer and something to back up your files (such as a flash drive or CD-RW).

Many computers already have the basic software needed to run a business. Some versions of Microsoft Office come with a whole suite of small business tools. You may also want to get a bookkeeping program such as Quicken or Quickbooks as well as a program to help you keep track of your clients.

For basic computer equipment and software, the staff at a computer store or your office supplies store can give you more information and help you decide which products are best for you.

Concierge Software

There isn't much software available designed specifically for a personal concierge business. Most software that is available has been designed for use by hotels, resorts, cruise lines and so on. However, there are a great number of client management-type software programs available. Some are available for online use so that you don't even have to install any software. FreeCRM.com is one example of this.

Database programs can help you to keep track of clients and the tasks associated with them. Popular programs in this category include Sage ACT! and FileMaker Pro. Microsoft Office Home and Business also includes a database program.

- *Filemaker Pro*
  www.filemaker.com/products/filemaker-pro

- *Sage ACT!*
  www.act.com

- *MS Office Home and Business*
  http://office.microsoft.com/en-us/home-and-business

Fax Machine and Photocopier

These used to be considered optional equipment for small businesses. But today, when you can get a unit that is a combination photocopier, fax machine, scanner, and printer for a few hundred dollars, you should consider getting one.

You are unlikely to need dozens of photocopies; you might need to make a copy or two of an agreement from time to time, and if you have the equipment right there, you won't have to go all the way to Kinko's to do it. And remember, time is money, especially when you have a lot to do and a lot on your mind.

File Cabinet

You'll need to keep files for each client. Your desk may have drawers that can hold files, but you will probably eventually need a file cabinet. Your options include two-door or four-door filing cabinets, or you may find a lateral file cabinet fits better with the rest of your office furniture.

Telephone and Fax

The number of different telephone plans is almost endless, but there are steps that you can take to keep everything fairly simple. If you choose to work out of your home, you probably do not even need to make any changes to your current telephone service. You will generally know when clients are calling, as you have already pre-arranged the times with them. You can install a separate business line, subscribe to Caller ID, or even get a different ring for when a client calls.

You'll also need a cell phone. This is an absolutely essential piece of equipment for a busy concierge, since you'll often be on the road and clients and service partners will still need to reach you. You might choose something like a BlackBerry or iPhone or some other type of phone that includes extra capabilities like email, Internet access, address book, etc. Keep in mind that these are a bit more expensive than a basic cell phone.

To ensure professionalism consider making your main office phone number a business line. You don't want your six-year-old picking up on a client calling in, after all. That just doesn't come across as very professional.

A business line will cost a little more than a residential line, but you will be listed under your business name in the white pages and with directory assistance, which makes it easier for clients to find you. You can also get a listing in the Yellow Pages under "Concierge Services" (or whatever category personal concierges are listed under in your local Yellow Pages).

Make this phone off-limits to the rest of the family. Always be sure it is answered professionally with a greeting that states your business name followed by "How can we help you?" These days, even large corporations have their phones answered by voice mail systems, so you might also want to install an answering machine or subscribe to the voicemail services offered by telephone companies.

Although email has replaced fax machines in most cases, you might still want to be able to send and receive faxes, particularly if you market yourself to executives or businesses. Rather than buy a fax machine, you might also consider an online service. eFax.com allows you to send and receive faxes through your email account for less than $20 per month. You can try it free for 30 days before subscribing.

4.6 Franchises

An alternative to starting your own business from scratch is to invest in a franchise. There are hundreds of franchise companies on the market today. Companies like Starbucks, McDonalds, and a host of others have had great success in convincing investors to buy into their business models. Many franchisees have themselves become millionaires as a result of running successful franchises.

As a franchisee, you will still own your own business but there is theoretically less risk involved for you because you are using someone else's proven business model. A franchisor is a company that has developed a successful system of operations, marketing, and service delivery. In exchange for using their business model, you will pay an initial franchise fee, as well as a percentage of your earnings to the franchisor and possibly some additional fees for programs like advertising campaigns.

In a sense, running a franchise is a mix of being an entrepreneur and being an employee. Because you set your own work hours and take care of all the day-to-day operations of your company, you're an entrepreneur. Because you work according to someone else's company policies, pay a percentage to them, use their marketing strategies, and ultimately answer to them for the success of your enterprise, it's a bit like being an employee. Still, you do have a certain degree of autonomy within those boundaries.

Note: The following discussion about franchises is for information purposes only. Neither FabJob nor the author endorses any franchise mentioned in this guide. Only you can decide whether or not a franchise is right for you.

Here is one example of a franchise available to you:

Cybertary

Description:	Cybertary is a company offering on-demand virtual assistant support services to companies. They specialize in office support services like desktop publishing, editing, marketing materials, executive assistance, meeting planning, concierge services, bookkeeping, invoicing, and more.
Address:	1217 Pleasant Grove Blvd, Suite 100 Roseville, CA 95678
Phone:	(888) 292-8279
Contact:	**www.cybertaryfranchise.com/learn-more**
Website:	**www.cybertaryfranchise.com**
Franchise Fee:	$37,500-$56,250 for a single-office setup and 5% royalty
Initial Investment:	$39,500-$78,500

There are franchises available in other related industries like event planning, childcare, party planning, travel/destination services, and so on. You can visit franchise websites such as **www.thefranchisemall.com** or **www.franchisemarketplace.com** to find out if one of these interests you.

Another good resource to look at if you're thinking of investing in a franchise is the franchise section on the Canada Business website. It gives you valuable tips on what to look for in a franchise company that will help you evaluate the merits of making such an investment. Visit **www.canadabusiness.ca/eng/guide/2014** for more information.

5. Running a Personal Concierge Business

5.1 Client Consultations

Your initial contact with clients may come by phone, by email, or in person. Although simple requests can be handled without meeting a client face to face, an in-person meeting is often necessary to help you determine how to best serve the regular client's needs.

This initial meeting can be an important part of the process of landing a new client. Especially if they have never had a personal concierge at their service before, your prospective client may have common misperceptions, such as the following:

- "Only extremely rich people hire help."

- "It's lazy/snobbish to have someone else do your work."

- "I don't have anything I need help with right now."

- "It's more work to explain how I want things done than to do it myself."

- "I don't have time to explain what I need."

- "I don't know what a personal concierge does."

- "Hiring help means I'm admitting I'm not capable."

- "It doesn't cost me anything if I do these things myself."

- "I'd rather not have a stranger involved in my personal life."

- "These are tasks that only I can do right."

In the initial meeting, you are going to set these fears to rest. You want your clients to walk away thinking about what great value you provide, how you nearly seem to read their minds, and that things are about to get better for them… with your help.

Personal concierge Jill Burstein shares the following spiel about the benefits of using a personal concierge for grocery shopping, with points you may want to share with clients to seal the deal:

"Consider the time it takes you to go grocery shopping, come home, and put it away. How many items were impulse-buys? Did you even have a list? What did you forget that you will have to go back to the store and get in midweek?

"If you have a concierge or errand person, they will start to know your brands and favorites — when I see a particular brand of hard-to-find canned spaghetti, I grab it for my client whether it's on the list or not. The time-factor alone is a huge selling point, even if you only use a concierge once or twice."

5.1.1 Assessing Clients' Needs

At your first meeting with a client you'll gather information on the concierge services that are needed, and get a big-picture idea of the client and his or her lifestyle. After you have identified what the client wants, then you can explain what services you offer, and how you can meet their needs.

Start by getting to know a bit about your client. Let the client do the talking as much as possible. Ask questions, and listen to what the answers reveal about the person's organizational skills, their current work load, and their work-life balance. Ask a few questions about how they use their spare time, their hobbies, and their family life. You'll come back to this when you present the value you are offering them, including more time for these things.

You can use the sample questionnaire on the next page to determine what areas of their lives clients need help with. Listen not only to the client's direct responses to these questions, but also to any details they add in themselves. If you want, you can ask the client to jot down answers to these questions before you meet so you can review them in person.

Once your clients have described some of the challenges they are experiencing, you can show them how you can help them find more time in their day. You'll match their greatest needs with services you provide.

It might be tempting to solve all your client's problems at once, but it's important to prioritize. Overwhelming clients with information and options is the same as becoming another item on their to-do list: "#77: Figure out best way to use personal concierge service."

Make the decision a simple one for them. Focus on one or two tasks you can start with, and grow from there. They need to see how you benefit their lives before opening the door the entire way to you. Don't lose a client because they don't get around to figuring out what to ask you to do.

> **TIP:** Take advantage of laptops and PowerPoint software to develop a presentation of what you can do for a client. You can take a PowerPoint training course at almost any community college.

It's important to keep an open mind and do your best work when dealing with any client, as you never know how future needs will change. Personal concierge Elyse Coleman of Life/Time CEO shares a story

Prospective Client Questionnaire

1. What is your typical day like from start to finish?

   _____

   _____

2. What does your to-do list look like right now?

   _____

   _____

3. What domestic or professional tasks are taking away time from your day?

   _____

   _____

4. What tasks or activities do you not enjoy or find yourself putting off?

   _____

   _____

5. What important parts of your life do you feel are currently neglected?

   _____

   _____

6. What would you do if you had eight free hours with no interruptions?

   _____

   _____

7. How would you use those eight hours differently if your to-do list was completed?

   _____

   _____

8. What do you hope or expect a personal concierge will do for you?

   _____

   _____

about how an apparent one-time client surprised her with a follow-up request:

> "A request came from a woman in Vancouver, BC who wanted Thanksgiving dinner delivered to her boyfriend, who lives here in my area. I recommended a local grocery store for her to order the dinner from, and I picked it up and delivered it. I thought it would be a one-off kind of thing and would never hear from them again, but to my delight, he recently called me to run errands for his mother and grandmother because he is out of town."

Remember that client meetings are a two-way street, and you don't have to take all clients. If someone seems overly picky about how you do your work, concerned about how you spend each minute, or generally unappreciative of you and your service, it may be time to end the relationship (or not start it at all). Perhaps you have a colleague who does better with that type of client, to whom you can refer them. Better now than having the negativity draining your energy.

5.1.2   Information to Collect

Once a client is sold on your service, you'll need to collect the information that will help you do your job. This information will vary depending on what tasks the client needs your help with. That is, you don't need their shoe size if they only want their dry cleaning dropped off. Still, gather as much information as is practical, in case your services expand down the road.

Once you have decided the services your client will benefit from, you need to determine how and when you will provide them. Do they want the groceries unloaded and put into the cupboards, or just dropped off to them? What days do they want you to complete regular tasks? You may want to develop a schedule of tasks that need doing frequently, such as grocery shopping or car washing.

You'll also want to get a sense of how often the client wants to be contacted by you, or if they would prefer to call you on an as-needed basis. You may find that this changes over time as the client becomes more confident in delegating tasks to you. At this same time, you'll want to let clients know what you expect of them, as explained in the next section on contracts.

Building a Client Database

Your basic client data to collect will include names (with proper spellings) of all family members and close extended family, birth dates, wedding anniversaries, clothing sizes of anyone you'll be shopping for, their employers and type of work they do, and what their hobbies are.

Get as many contact numbers as possible for your client, including work, home, vacation home, and cell, and an email address. You'll also need to know if there are family pets, and if they are friendly (or will be crated) if you need to get into the house.

Your extended information to collect will cover favorites and preferences to help you make decisions like your client: favorite foods, music, movies, sports, restaurants, and even favorite colors. Don't forget that Chapter 2 of this guide has many more questions for you to use with your clients, geared towards specific services you may provide.

Your client information should be added to with every service request or project you complete for them. Since this can amount to fair bit of paperwork when it comes to regular clients, consider using software like Microsoft Outlook or FileMaker Pro (**www.filemaker.com**) to create a client contact database and make notes.

5.1.3   Engagement Letters and Contracts

In many service businesses, contracts with individual clients take the form of letters of agreement, also known as engagement letters. Formal contracts, also known as service agreements, are more commonly used when you are agreeing to perform services for a corporation and/or its employees.

What to Include

These documents spell out what services you will provide for the client, when you will provide them (the dates between which or by which your services are to be completed), as well as when and how you are to be paid.

Any agreement or contract should include your company name and address, as well as the name and address of your client. And of course, they should be signed by both parties. Your own agreement may also add:

- A cancellation policy (for both when you have to cancel, and when your client needs to cancel on you)
- A confidentiality policy
- Services you exclude or don't perform
- Any authorizations (such as use of credit card or to let contractors in)
- A statement of fees
- A limitation of liability
- Terms for terminating the agreement

On the pages that follow you will find two samples which you can adapt to fit your needs. The first is a sample engagement letter you might use with an individual client. You could ask your clients to sign it at your initial meeting, or have them return it to you later.

The second is a services agreement which you could adapt for use with a corporate client. It covers a number of additional areas, such as a product/service liability disclaimer so that you cannot be held responsible for defects in items you buy or services you subcontract for your clients.

Make sure you have any contract or agreement reviewed by a lawyer. Doing so now could save you the services of a lawyer later on. Even with engagement letters, ask your lawyer about including additional clauses to protect you, such as a limitation of liability clause (see the sample services agreement for an example).

Standard Engagement Letter

(On Your Letterhead)

[Insert name of Client]

[Insert address of Client]

[Date]

Dear *[Name of client]*,

As promised, I have set out below a description of the services that *[your name/concierge company name]* will provide to you.

I will provide the following services:

[Insert description of the services: running errands, grocery shopping, house sitting, etc.] and other services as agreed by the client and *[your name/concierge company name]*.

Please note that I will not be providing these services:

[Insert description of the services that will not be provided, e.g. child care]

In order for me to carry out the services you will:
[Insert anything you require the client to do or provide before you can carry out the service. For example, if they need to tell their condominium association that you are authorized to carry out household repairs on your client's behalf.]

My fee for the services performed will be as follows:

[Insert rates] plus expenses. *[Insert your payment policy, e.g. Before services are performed you will provide me with a deposit for the estimated cost. The balance will be paid or refunded upon completion of the service.]*

If scheduled services are cancelled by the client for any reason less than *[insert your cancellation deadline, such as 48 hours before the date scheduled]*, a cancellation fee of *[insert amount such as $25, 10%, etc.]* is payable to *[your name/concierge company name]*.

If you agree that the foregoing fairly sets out your understanding of our mutual responsibilities, please sign a copy of this letter in the space indicated below, and return it to me at *[insert address, fax number or email address]*.

Yours sincerely,
[Name]

Agreed and Accepted:

_____
[Insert name of client]

_____
[Date]

Sample Services Agreement

THIS AGREEMENT is made this *[date]* day of *[month]*, 20__.

BETWEEN
[insert client's name] (the "Client"); and *[insert your name or your company's name]* (the "Concierge Service"), collectively referred to as the "Parties."

1.1 Services

The Concierge Service shall provide the following services ("Services") to the Client in accordance with the terms and conditions of this Agreement: *[Insert a description of the services here]*.

1.2 Delivery of the Services

Start date: The Concierge Service shall commence the provision of the Services on *[insert date here]*.

Completion date: The Concierge Service shall complete the Services by *[insert date here]* ("Completion Date").

1.3 Fees

As consideration for the provision of the Services by the Concierge Service, the fees for the provision of the Services are *[insert fees here]* ("Fees"). The Client shall pay for the Concierge Service's out-of-pocket expenses including *[insert here]* and other expenses as agreed by the Parties.

1.4 Payment

The Client agrees to pay the Fees to the Concierge Service on the following dates: *[e.g. 50% deposit payable before work begins; also specify whether fees will be paid monthly or upon completion of specific services]*.

The Concierge Service shall invoice the Client for the Services that it has provided to the Client each month. The Client shall pay such invoices *[upon receipt / within 30 days of receipt]* from the Concierge Service.

Any charges payable under this Agreement are exclusive of any applicable taxes or other fees charged by a government body and such shall be payable by the Client to the Concierge Service in addition to all other charges payable hereunder.

1.5 Warranty

The Concierge Service represents and warrants that it will perform the Services with reasonable skill and care.

1.6 Limitation of Liability

Subject to the Client's obligation to pay the Fees to the Concierge Service, either Party's liability arising directly out of its obligations under this Agreement and every applicable part of it shall be limited in aggregate to the Fees. The Consultant assumes no liability due to the quality of items or services purchased for the Client.

1.7 Term and Termination

This Agreement shall be effective on the date hereof and shall continue until the completion date stated in section 1.2 unless terminated sooner. If the Client terminates this agreement for any reason before the scheduled completion date, the Client will reimburse the Concierge Service for all outstanding fees and out-of-pocket expenses.

1.8 Relationship of the Parties

The Parties acknowledge and agree that the Services performed by the Concierge Service, its employees, sub-contractors, or agents shall be as an independent contractor and that nothing in this Agreement shall be deemed to constitute a partnership, joint venture, or otherwise between the Parties.

1.9 Confidentiality

Neither Party will disclose any information of the other which comes into its possession under or in relation to this Agreement and which is of a confidential nature.

1.10 Miscellaneous

The failure of either Party to enforce its rights under this Agreement at any time for any period shall not be construed as a waiver of such rights.

If any part, term or provision of this Agreement is held to be illegal or unenforceable neither the validity or enforceability of the remainder of this Agreement shall be affected.

This Agreement constitutes the entire understanding between the Parties and supersedes all prior representations, negotiations or understandings.

Neither Party shall be liable for failure to perform any obligation under this Agreement if the failure is caused by any circumstances beyond its reasonable control, including but not limited to acts of god, war, or industrial dispute.

This Agreement shall be governed by the laws of the jurisdiction in which the Client is located.

Agreed by the Parties hereto:

Signed by: _____

On behalf of: _____
[the Client]

Signed by: _____

On behalf of: _____
[the Concierge Service]

5.2 Setting Your Fees

What you charge clients will be based on your local market and economy, what other personal concierges are charging, and the quality and type of service that you offer. This section will look at ways to help you determine what to charge clients and the different ways to charge fees, as well as how to collect when money is due.

5.2.1   Factors That Affect Pricing

To set your fees, you'll want to start by taking a look at what other concierge services charge. But it's not as simple as making those your same fees too. While charging the same as other concierge services makes sense on the surface, it doesn't factor in how your business may be different. For example, you may have more or less overhead, a wealthier clientele, specialized services, or different profit goals than your competitors.

"I did Internet searches for rates all over the country, and wrote them down. Then I tried to judge what would fly in my neck of the woods," says Jill Burstein about her personal concierge business, which services the metro Detroit area. "I have doubled my rate since inception, and

with gas costing more and more, I can see my rates going up again soon," she adds.

To determine how your fees should stack up, you need to figure out approximately how much it's going to cost you to provide your service. Use the typical expenses listed in section 4.1.2, and calculate your approximate monthly overhead. Calculate gasoline expense based on the number of clients you would ideally like to have.

The figure you come up with is your break-even point, and the minimum you can earn monthly to stay in business. It's unlikely that you will earn this much in your first, second or third months of business. In fact, many businesses report a loss in their first year of operation. But with the help of an accountant, you'll be able to work out a projection of how you'll show a profit in time.

When you look for competitors to base your prices on, look to those operating in similar geographic and economic conditions for a realistic comparison. In general, businesses in smaller towns charge less than urban services, but your costs of doing business and living generally will be higher in an urban center. For example, you might pay $10 to park downtown and run errands in a big city, but have access to free street parking in a small town.

The type of client you are serving may also be a factor in your pricing. It makes sense that one-time or infrequent clients will pay more to have you drop everything and assist them, while regular clients, or corporate clients who retain you for a number of employees (especially those who prepay or book in advance) can be offered a discount based on the volume of work they generate.

Some personal concierges will charge different fees based on the service they are providing. Planning a lavish party, with all its many details, may seem in your mind (and your clients' minds) to merit a higher fee than waiting for the cable guy to show up. Just be warned that billing this way may confuse your clients, and it also opens the door to debate on what each of your services are worth. It may be easier to have a standard rate for your time, regardless of the task.

Competing on Price

If you want to compete with other personal concierges on price, that's fine. Many do, especially when they first enter the market. But there is great danger in taking a survey of what the competition is charging, and then setting your prices at, say, ten percent below the going rate.

Think about it — your competitors, if they're smart, took a look at their expenses, and then set a reasonable rate for their expertise and time, in order to ensure that they made the profit they required. By charging lower than that, there's a good chance that you will be running a business that loses money.

If you are planning on pricing yourself low, you'll need to run at a higher volume, meaning more hours worked. If you price yourself in the high range, you'll need to provide exceptional service that merits the cost, but can get away with fewer hours worked overall. If it works out that you can charge less and still operate as a success, then by all means go for it. But know that you have to set your prices based on your own breakeven.

5.2.2   Ways to Charge Your Fees

By the Hour

Most personal concierge services charge for time by the hour, although there are some variations to be explained further on in this section. Basically, you keep track of the number of hours you do work for a client, and bill the client for those hours at a set rate.

Based on research and interviews for this guide, an average rate for personal concierge services in North America currently is about $40 an hour. A survey of what hourly rate five real personal concierge services charge showed a fair amount of variance, and rose corresponding with the local population:

- Sample A: $25 an hour in a city of 450,000

- Sample B: $30 an hour in a city of 1.2 million

- Sample C: $35 an hour in a county of 3 million

- Sample D: $55 an hour in a city of 3.5 million

- Sample E: $55 - $85 an hour in a city of 5 million

Billing by the hour typically starts once you are "on the clock." So for example, you would not charge for your time to drive to a client's house to work on an organizing project, but would commence billing once you arrive. Similarly, billing time would end when you left for home or the next client, although you would likely round up to the nearest half-hour or hour.

On the other hand, if a client asks you to pick up a bracelet at her aunt's house and bring it to her at work, you could certainly justify charging billable time as soon as you leave your home. Just make sure that your reasoning of how you charge your clients is both logical and consistent.

Based on how your business grows or the market responds, you may have to raise or lower prices accordingly. "[At first] I cruised the web for what others were charging... but I've adjusted since then, and lowered my prices," says Bev Riggins of Midwest Concierge Service.

> **TIP:** It is advisable to charge a one- or two-hour minimum to your clients, so your time deciding how to complete a task and travel to your client is covered. That way if a client asked you to come and change a light bulb, they wouldn't expect to pay you only for the minute it took to climb a ladder and do the job.

Another pricing consideration is overtime pricing. If you will be working Monday through Friday, for example, you could charge a higher rate for any services provided on weekends. So, if you normally charge $35 per hour through the week, you could charge $55 per hour on weekends. Similarly, if you have set hours of operation, such as 9:00 a.m. to 7:00 p.m., you could charge at a higher rate before or after that time period.

Charging for Expenses

You can charge for expenses involved in providing services to your clients. For example, if you have to pay for parking when you're running errands, you can have the client reimburse you for that expense.

Due to the high price of gas, many personal concierge and/or errand services also charge mileage over a certain number of miles — typically 5 to 10, depending on how far-flung your city or town is. "I charge mileage based on the [2011] IRS rate of 44.5 cents per mile, and it is charged to the client based on mileage that exceeds 10 miles," says Delmar Johnson of The Concierge Place.

The idea is that basic travel to and from the client is your expense, but any driving you do on their behalf is theirs. Again, this covers your cost if a client wants you to shop at a specialty vendor on the outskirts of the city, instead of the Costco down the block.

> **TIP:** Make sure you keep track of all your expenses so you can get reimbursed for them. For mileage, keep a careful mileage log of all driving you do for work. While you will bill client miles directly, all other mileage can count towards income tax deductions. Depending on how much they are, you may wish to charge clients for road tolls as well, or absorb them yourself. Consult an accountant on the best way to arrange this for your business.

In addition to charging for expenses, you'll need to charge the client for any taxes that are required to be collected by your local, state or provincial, or federal governments. For example, in Canada, businesses that earn over $30,000 per year are required to charge their clients a 6% Goods and Services Tax. See section 4.3.3 for information about taxes and resources to help you determine taxes related to your own concierge business.

Discounts and Premiums

If you want to encourage people to try your services for the first time, you can offer a cheaper rate for the first few hours of service. Just be clear with them that it is a one-time discount, and that your regular rates will apply in the future. The initial consultation when you explain your services is usually offered free of charge.

As mentioned earlier, you can discount prepaid hours for your clients if you want. For example, your fees could be $45 an hour, or $120 for three prepaid hours (a discount of $15, or $5 an hour). Prepaid hours are great because they are guaranteed income, and they help your cash flow.

Depending on your lifestyle and other commitments, you may want to specify that your hourly rates apply only to regular business hours, or state strictly the hours you are available. If you are available for service calls after hours, you can either charge a premium for after-hours requests, or charge a monthly retainer to clients who prefer to have you available around the clock.

Memberships

Some concierge services also offer a membership option for their clients. Under this arrangement, clients receive additional member benefits that non-members don't receive. Obviously, if someone wants to become a member they are planning to use your services on a regular basis, and you are offering them these benefits based on the increased patronage.

Generally in this type of arrangement, clients sign up as members for a set amount. You could also charge a graded membership fee, such as Silver, Gold, and Platinum. This could be a few hundred dollars to a thousand dollars or more, depending on the number of services you offer and the types of services clients will have access to.

Membership benefits could include things like discounts on the hourly rate normally charged, preferential services (i.e. members have priority over non-members), additional services not offered to non-members, and so on. You might not be able to implement this type of layered pricing right away, but as you build your business and find additional partner companies, such as limo services, hotels, restaurants, florists, etc., this might be an option to consider.

A La Carte Services

Certain services you offer, where it's pretty easy to gauge the amount of work involved, can be billed a la carte, meaning a flat rate for a certain service. Think of house sitting, gift wrapping or dog walking as typical examples. They should be services that are used frequently by many of your clients, to justify having a separate price for them, or services that are nice lead-ins you don't mind taking a bit of a loss on (versus your regular hourly rate) to bring you new clients.

"I use a flat fee," says Jill Burstein of Jill will... Concierge Service. "I like it for a lot of reasons. I find I don't have to answer for my hours and can ethically juggle several clients at the same time if I am not billing by the hour. It's simple too, and I like simple," she adds.

If you have specialized skills such as computer repair, graphic design, or website management, you can either charge these services at a higher a la carte rate than your other basic services, or bill them the same and use them as value-added features to attract more clients — when you are first starting out, having more clients on board may bring you the greater value of the two.

Service Packages

Packaging services to sell offers some distinct advantages for the personal concierge. First, it may allow you to boost your earnings. A Holiday Decorating Package you offer, complete with steaming hot chocolate waiting for your clients when they arrive home and holiday music playing, is hopefully more appealing than simply stating that you can put up their holiday lights.

Packaging services also opens clients' minds to the idea of using your services as a thoughtful or seasonal gift. Offer gift certificates in designated blocks of time or packages of services, as opposed to dollar amounts that put an exact value on the gift. "I like to sell a block of time, with no expiration of when it can be used," says Bev Riggins of Midwest Concierge Service.

Packaging your most commonly used concierge services may also help reluctant clients understand better what you can do for them. Telling a client you can do "anything, any time they ask," is kind of vague, and really doesn't help you close a deal. Telling them instead that they can start with a basic service package that includes weekly meal planning, grocery shopping, and dry cleaning drop off/pick-up gives them something concrete to say "yes" to.

Once a client makes you a part of his or her life, you're more likely to find the hours go up from there. Be creative with your package offerings — really try to get into the minds of your clients and think about what will motivate them to call you. You can survey other personal concierges for inspiration, either by sharing ideas on online forums or taking a look at a variety of websites.

Corporate Pricing

When you are hired on as a personal concierge for a business or corporation, you typically charge the company a monthly retainer. A monthly retainer is a fee that clients pay you on a monthly basis. In return, you agree to be available for a particular number of hours of work each month.

Steady income like this is good for your business, as it can be relied upon every month. It is also good for your client, because it ensures they have a concierge service available to them every month on an on-going basis, usually for a lower cost than it would cost the company to hire a full-time employee.

A retainer arrangement may be made for any period of time acceptable to both you and the client. For example, you might work on retainer for a period of six months, a year, or longer. If a retainer arrangement is renewed, it might be for the same fee or you might renegotiate the fee or number of hours.

A retainer fee is usually based on how many employees the company has, or how often service requests are expected. The fee may start at several hundred dollars per month and go up from there. An article in the *Toronto Star* newspaper reported that "Concierge companies typically receive a monthly retainer of several thousand dollars."

On top of the retainer, you might still charge an hourly rate when you do work for the employees, although this rate may be lower than your direct-to-client service fee. Who pays your hourly rate depends on the program the employer has set up. Some employers subsidize a set number of service hours per employee, while others leave the charge for service to the employee.

The employees are also responsible for paying for the actual products or services you provide for them. For example, if you pick up dry cleaning and get concert tickets for an employee, the employee pays for the dry cleaning and tickets, not the employer.

Another take on corporate pricing is a personal concierge "member-ship." No retainer is necessarily required, but you become the exclu-sive provider of concierge services to anyone associated with a certain group, such as condominium owners or golf club members. You can of-fer a slightly discounted rate to the group in exchange for direct promo-tion to their members. This type of program is an easier sell to groups or companies than a program they have to pay for, but the drawback to you is that there is no guarantee you will ever get any income out of the arrangement.

When personal concierge expenses are covered by the company, you'll generally be dealing with more clients who use you less frequently, and you won't be able to collect immediately when you provide service. Make sure that you have a) the ability to handle the volume of service requests, and b) the cash flow to front expenses until you are paid — usually at month's end.

5.2.3 Getting Paid

When you are running your personal concierge service, you'll want to be paid as quickly as possible for the services you provide. To ac-complish this, two ways you can consider are: 1) requiring a deposit or prepayment for service, or 2) requiring payment immediately after the service is rendered.

Depending on the client and the service, either of these options may be appropriate. For example, it would be difficult for a client to prepay the exact amount of a grocery bill, but if they write you a check to cover the approximate amount, you can bill them the balance at a later time. Sim-ilarly, if a client is not home, they can't write you a check for awaiting a service provider. But perhaps they will allow you to bill their credit card when you get back to the office.

For clients who are (or who want to become regulars), you can ask them to buy blocks of time in advance. You'll need to keep careful records, and report the balance to your clients when money is debited. "Most clients prepay," says Bev Riggins of Midwest Concierge Service. "If I purchase items, I either pay for them and get reimbursed, or use a pre-purchased gift card."

What you have to do is work out a system for payment that works with your client's availability and lifestyle, and makes sure that you get paid in a timely manner. You can't wait for all your clients to pay you at month's end unless you have an excellent cash flow. Invoicing after the fact will also make calling and collecting payment part of your to-do list, which is time you are not earning.

> **TIP:** Avoid fronting the cost of third-party services for your clients. You may be okay with the occasional small amount to bill back to them, but don't carry their debt. It may also drag you into any disputes about the payment or quality of work.

When billing your clients or providing a receipt, you will need to carefully itemize your charges, including materials you buy on their behalf, expenses you incurred, mileage, and taxes paid on their behalf or that they must pay. They should be able to see exactly what the charges are for, and what their opening/closing balances were if they have prepaid.

"The Concierge Place is set up to accept cash and checks in person and credit cards via PayPal, and is structured as a pre-paid service provider. Billing for items purchased is estimated and established at the time a service request is made by a client, and pre-paid," says Delmar Johnson.

If you want to accept payment by credit card, you need to set up a merchant account with your bank. Increasingly, small businesses are turning to online payment options (like PayPal) as a way to cut the fees of a merchant account. Just make sure the payment option you choose is secure and still convenient for you and your clients. For information visit **www.paypal.com**.

Personal concierge Jill Burstein explains billing and payment with her corporate accounts: "I invoice them monthly for the time I work. And I have the corporation's credit cards on file as well. If I am buying them supplies at Sam's Club or Costco, I pay upfront and deliver the goods, then later in the day, I charge their account. Today alone, I fronted about $500 in transactions, only to get the money back later in the day by charging their accounts."

Invoicing Corporate Clients

If you are charging corporate clients a monthly retainer, you will likely submit monthly invoices to the client. A challenge with invoicing is that corporations normally expect at least 30 days to pay, and some wait longer before putting a check in the mail. So it's a good idea to ask for a deposit up front.

For example, if you have a year-long contract where the fee is on a monthly retainer basis, you could ask to be paid up front for the first month. So if the monthly retainer is $2,500, you could ask for a deposit of $2,500 before beginning work.

Your invoice should be on your letterhead and include the following items:

- The client name and contact information
- A purchase order number (if the client gave you one)
- A list of services you provided with the date and cost

- Any expenses and taxes payable

- The total amount due

- Terms of payment (e.g. "Payable upon receipt" or "Payable within 30 days")

Sample Invoice

(On Your Letterhead)

DATE: July 30, 2013

TO: [Client name and address]

RE: Concierge Services for the Month of July, 2013

FEES:

   Retainer Fee (as per contract of May 7, 2013)......$3,000.00

   Tax on Retainer Fee (*Insert your own local tax rate*) $300.00

   Expenses (receipts enclosed)....................................$126.58

   Mileage...$44.50

   Parking $33.29

   Courier Charges...$48.79

   TOTAL – PLEASE PAY THIS AMOUNT........................**$3,553.16**

TERMS: Payable upon receipt.

Thank you for your business.

5.3 Working with Service Providers and Vendors

Service providers are individuals and companies that you hire to provide additional services to your clients. Vendors are companies that sell either products or services.

When you run a personal concierge business, your clients will rely on you to have a network of professional, responsible service providers you can call to do great work, and even work the occasional miracle.

The trick is to have many of these relationships in place before you start working with clients. Of course you will meet many service providers on the job, but you'll want to be somewhat established at the outset. Keep your list of contacts with you at all times — you never know when you'll need to make that call.

5.3.1   When Is It Best to Outsource?

When you first start up your personal concierge service, it may be a challenge to decide when to hire a professional, and when to do hands-on work yourself. Ask yourself the following questions when you are debating whether or not to outsource a particular task:

- Do I have the requirements (insurance, skills) to do this task?
- Do I need the hours this week/month, or am I booked up?
- Does this task need to be done immediately, or can it wait?
- Do I know someone who can do this better/faster than I can?
- Does this task require my personal touch?
- Is there a good reason I should (or should not) take this task on?

Many personal concierges will always outsource driving and childcare, to avoid extra charges on their insurance. Services like housekeeping and gardening are also typically outsourced, since your hourly fee is usually well beyond what it would cost the client to hire a specialized service for these tasks. Personal concierge Jill Burstein adds event planning to the list of jobs she prefers not to tackle.

"In my opinion, the three best outsourced requests include transport services, pet sitting, and event planning — particularly if you have not planned an event before. I would go a little further and suggest that you concentrate on those areas that you have narrowed down as your niche markets, and work those to excellence," says personal concierge Delmar Johnson.

Remember that as a personal concierge, you are a manager, not a servant. You are paid to determine the best way to get things done for your client. If someone needs to plant flowers next week, a gardening service can be called. If those flowers need to be planted today, it's time for you to break out the gardening gloves and knee pads. And some tasks will simply require your own personal touch to be done to the client's specifications.

The tendency with new concierge businesses is to do more of the work hands-on, and gradually outsource more and more as you build your clientele. This way you get work-hours when you need them, and turn into more of a facilitator as your time becomes booked up. Also remember that if you are trying to do everything yourself, that's time you are not landing new clients or generating more business, which can also be detrimental to the new concierge.

5.3.2   Finding Service Providers/Vendors

Contacts to Have in Place

Here is a list of service providers and vendors you will refer to most often for your clients. You should have a preferred contact in place for each, as well as some options if they can't meet your request:

Sample Contact List

❑ Accountant

❑ Architectural designer

❑ Business consultant

❑ Caterer

❑ Computer expert

❑ Copywriter

❑ Custom framing

❑ Daycare or nanny service

❑ Dry cleaning service

- ❑ Electrician
- ❑ Etiquette consultant
- ❑ Florist
- ❑ Graphic designer
- ❑ Handyman
- ❑ Home stager
- ❑ Housekeeping service
- ❑ Interior decorator
- ❑ Landscape company
- ❑ Lawyer (various types)
- ❑ Mechanic
- ❑ Other personal concierges
- ❑ Party planner
- ❑ Personal chef
- ❑ Personal shopper
- ❑ Personal trainer
- ❑ Plumber
- ❑ Professional organizer
- ❑ Realtor
- ❑ Tailor
- ❑ Taxi and/or limo service
- ❑ Temp agency
- ❑ Travel consultant
- ❑ Web designer
- ❑ Veterinary service

Keep an ongoing list of service providers or vendors to research, and schedule appointments with them when you are not busy. Use the techniques explained in the next section to evaluate them. When you are satisfied, add them to your ongoing list. Remove those who disappoint you or your clients even once without a good explanation.

Researching Service Providers/Vendors

You will be judged by the level of service that your service providers give to your clients, so you will want to select those that you work or partner with, with care. If you are going to approach them directly, be prepared to explain who you are and what you do. You are in a position to refer them frequently, so you should receive a warm response.

You can ask other personal concierges or related service professionals (e.g., wedding planners, professional organizers, home stagers) for referrals to the vendors they use. If that service provider has been in business for a while, chances are that their vendors are the best out there. If you want to attract vendors or service providers, you can include an application form on your website.

Your evaluation process for contractors for your business or your clients should include asking to see a valid business license and proof of insurance or bonding if required. You may also want to turn to the Better Business Bureau, and call references that the business is able to provide. If they have a place of business, drop by unannounced. Listen to how they interact with their own clients.

In person or over the phone, inquire about things that will be good to know about their business or service in advance, such as return or service policies, average turnaround time, specializations, and price. Record regular business hours, and see if they are willing to provide an after-hours contact. List this information in a spreadsheet you can refer to. If you are a member of PersonalAssistantPro.com, a chart you can use is available in their download library.

5.3.3   Hiring and Paying Service Providers and Vendors

Your relationship with your service providers and vendors can be whatever you want.

One option is to arrange the service for your client under the umbrella of your concierge business. In that case the service provider is working for you rather than your client and would invoice your company. You in turn would invoice the client for the service as part of your fee. In this case, you would need to specify in your client contract that any such services would be billed in addition to your fee.

Although you might be out of pocket for a while until you are paid by the client, this option could ultimately be more profitable for you if you include the services at a price marked up to cover your overhead. For example, if the service provider charges you $100, you might charge the client a fee of $150 for that particular service. Alternatively, any preferred rates the vendor offers you could be passed along to clients as a perk of using your service.

Another option is to simply refer clients to deal directly with your preferred vendors. The vendors would then bill your client directly. That way you wouldn't risk being in the position where you have to pay the service provider's bill before you have been paid by the client.

Referral Fees

An increasingly common practice in business is the payment of "referral fees." For example, if you refer a client to a consultant, that vendor pays you a fee as a thank you for referring business to them that they otherwise would not have. Likewise, you could pay them a referral fee for any business they send your way.

There are no firm guidelines for the amount of a referral fee. It can be whatever you negotiate with a particular service provider, and might be a commission or percentage of what they earn from the referral (e.g. five percent to 20 percent) or a flat fee. In some cases, a service provider will not be willing to pay a referral fee (for example, if they are already booked up with work at their full fee). When you take on the role of coordinating the service and collecting payment, you might charge a higher referral fee, such as 25 percent of the cost of the services. This fee typically comes off what the service partner is paid, not added to the client's charge.

TIP: There is a degree of ethics involved in getting "kickbacks" from your vendors. If you refer a client to receive a fee, and the client finds out after the fact, the client may wonder if your referral was based on earning a few bucks, or if you genuinely had their best interests in mind. It's usually better to be on the level with your clients about commissions you will receive, or to pass along any discounts you receive directly to your clients.

If you have a referral fee arrangement with your strategic partners, it's wise to have a written agreement to protect yourself. Another situation where an agreement is needed is if you offer inclusive services or package deals for your clients with one price tag. In this situation, the client will pay you and you pay the providers.

If you do have a written agreement with a provider, make it as specific as possible. Outline exactly what services you are expecting and what the exact cost will be. Don't leave room for a service provider to add to their bottom line at your client's expense. This scenario shouldn't happen very often, though, because it will mean the end of your relationship with that provider who may be penny-wise but pound-foolish.

On the next two pages you will find a sample agreement. Make sure you consult with an attorney when preparing your own agreement to ensure it covers everything you need.

5.3.4   Strategic Partnerships

Arranging strategic partnerships with other service providers can be an effective way to win referrals for your own business. In this case, money doesn't change hands, but you simply refer business to each other as often as possible. This makes sense when you consider that a business may earn hundreds or even thousands of dollars from one referred client, so a kickback of $50 pales in comparison. Instead, it may be more valuable to you to get referrals for your own business.

You should always try to find a way to thank those who refer clients to you. Sometimes a phone call is enough — and sometimes a small gift is appropriate, depending on the value of the referral. Gifts can also be part of establishing a relationship with certain vendors. While not a bribe per se, it will help you be remembered fondly much more than a

Sample Agreement With Service Provider

1. Purpose of the Contract

[Your name/company name] (hereinafter called the "Concierge Service") hereby enters into a Contract with *[Name of Service Provider/Supplier/Contractor]* (hereinafter called the "Supplier" and collectively called the "Parties") to render services and/or provide goods for the benefit of the Concierge Service's client, *[Insert client's name]*, of *[Insert Client's address]*, (hereinafter called the "Client").

2. The Services

The Supplier shall provide the Client the following goods and services (the "Services") as directed by the Concierge Service:

[Insert description of services]

3. Length of Contract

The terms of this Contract shall be in effect from *[Insert start date]*, the Start Date, until completion of the Services on *[Insert end date]*, the Completion Date.

4. Fees and Payment

The Fees for the Services provided by the Supplier shall be:

[Insert prices and fees agreed to between you and the supplier]

The Supplier shall concurrently send invoices for work completed to the Client and to the Concierge Service within *[e.g. 7, 14, 30]* days of the Completion Date as agreed in section 3 ("Length of Contract") above.

Within 7 days of payment of the Fees by the Client for the Services provided by the Supplier, the Supplier shall pay to the Concierge Service ___% of the amount of the Fees as a referral fee.

5. Limit of Liability

Subject to the Supplier's obligation to provide the Services to the Client on behalf of the Concierge Service, either Party's liability arising directly out of its obligations under this Agreement and every applicable part of it shall be limited in aggregate to the Services provided.

Any goods provided or services undertaken by the Supplier, except those specified in section 2 ("The Services") above unless otherwise agreed to in writing, or without the express written consent of the Concierge Service shall be the sole responsibility of the Supplier. Any goods and services not expressly agreed to in writing between the Concierge Service and the Supplier shall be deemed outside the scope of this Contract, including, but not limited to, any liabilities, additional fees, or payments attached to or arising from the provision of such additional goods and services.

The Concierge Service shall not be responsible for payment(s) to the Supplier for the Services, nor for any disagreements arising from the Services as provided by the Supplier. The Supplier hereby acknowledges that the Client is solely responsible for Payment of the Services.

6. Entire Agreement

We, the undersigned, hereby acknowledge that this Contract represents the entire agreement between the Concierge Service and the Supplier, and that we are in agreement to the terms and conditions of this Contract:

Signature: _____   Date: _____
            (The Supplier)
Address: _____
Telephone: _____

Signature: _____   Date: _____
            (The Concierge Service)
Address: _____
Telephone: _____

business card. Raise the bar when you reward special services, such as short notice or those requiring overtime.

Keep in touch often with your service providers, even if you haven't used their services in a while. Let them know when you have referred a client, or ask referred clients to mention your name. Section 6.4.1 provides more information about getting referrals for your business.

5.4 Hiring Staff

Many personal concierge services start out as one-person operations. But even within one successful year of doing business, you may realize that, like your clients, you could be a lot more efficient if you had someone to help you out.

"A tipping point that would indicate a need for personnel is when you as the concierge begin to feel that you need a 'second you,' just like the clients you are servicing," says Delmar Johnson of The Concierge Place. "I think it's a good idea to bring someone else into the picture when you feel overburdened and find yourself not managing time as well as you did when you had fewer clients."

"I am there now," confesses one owner of a personal concierge business. "I find that my clients' needs are slipping through the cracks, or that I haven't invoiced or am too tired to bill."

When you are ready too, here are some guidelines for adding to your team.

5.4.1 Employees and Contractors

You have a few options when it comes to paying others to help free up your time.

You may hire your own personal assistant or concierge, or you might decide to hire general-assignment employees for your business. A third option is assigning individual contractors to take on specific tasks. One selection or a combination of these modes may be right for your business.

Hiring Employees

Hiring employees for your business is ideal in many ways. Employees do work assigned by you, and do it in a way that you determine. Employees are available for the hours they agree to work, and over time become better at tasks as you train them.

Good employees can be hard to find, though, and there's no guarantee that, after six months of teaching them all you know, they won't quit because they found something better — or worse, decide to run a competing business. Employees are also more costly to your business than the salary they get paid, as you will also contribute to their Social Security and/or pension funds, and cover their actions through your insurance.

If you hire employees, you'll need to define the scope of their work when you interview and hire them. As your assistant, an employee will expect to work directly for you. A general employee can work on tasks for you, as well as assignments for your clients (through you) when it makes sense. Guidelines for interviewing and evaluating employees follow in the next section. Nolo.com also has some useful information at **www.nolo.com/legal-encyclopedia/hiring-employees**.

Before deciding whether to hire employees, check with your local department of labor to find out all the rules and regulations required as an employer. There may be other state and federal rules and regulations that may apply to you, including: health and safety regulations, Workers' Compensation, minimum wage and unemployment insurance.

In addition to your local department of labor, visit these sites for more information:

- *U.S. Internal Revenue Service*
  (Search for "employees and contractors")
  www.irs.gov

- *U.S. Department of Labor*
  www.dol.gov/opa/aboutdol/lawsprog.htm

- *Canada Business Network*
  www.canadabusiness.ca/eng

Casual Employees and Contractors

You may be able to locate and retain people interested in part-time or casual employment, who will take assignments on call from you. Retirees, stay-at-home parents, and responsible university students are good candidates for casual employment. Depending on your local regulations, there may be a cap on the number of hours casual employees can work for you in a 12-month period without being considered regular employees.

Contractors are different from employees in that you don't invest time in training them, nor do they work hours specified by you. They are self-employed, and you pay them on an hourly or per-task basis to complete specific tasks. You may be interested in hiring contractors for specialized services, such as an accountant, business consultant, or PR specialist.

There are obvious benefits to having casuals or contractors instead of employees. They are usually less costly to your business than employees, since you don't need to pay the government on their behalf, and you pay them only for time spent completing a task. However, "casual" can work both ways, and you may find that your occasional helpers are not as dedicated as employees, don't complete tasks the way you want them to, or are simply unavailable when you need them.

Going on Your Own

If you decide not to hire any employees or casual subcontractors, you'll need to figure out a way to run your business very efficiently, and eventually put a cap on your number of clients or hours worked. It's easy to make the mistake of spreading yourself too thin, but in the end your lack of attention to detail, lack of availability, or even your lack of sleep trying to overdo it will cost you.

Free up your time by referring one-time clients to other personal concierges, or in some way taking on only your best clients. Working for fewer clients is usually more efficient than working for many. You can also boost your bottom line by cutting expenses like advertising, which aren't necessary when you're already swamped with business.

5.4.2   Interviews, Training and Pay

Here are some techniques you can use to help select honest, loyal employees and contractors who will be a great help to you in the same way you are for your clients:

- Look for employees who have skills that fill in areas where you may be lacking, or that complement your company's existing specialty. In general, good people/communication skills and being organized are two traits you want to see demonstrated in an interview.

- It's very important to select individuals for employment or contractors who will represent you and your business well. When you interview, picture this person out on the job. Consider appearance and attitude. Is this the public face you want for your business?

- Get a sense of their commitment to working with you. Students will usually only stay with you until they complete their studies — is that this spring? A resume with great credentials but a large number of jobs might suggest that this person does not last long in any position.

- Always check references. You might think that any reference listed would simply speak glowingly of the candidate, but you'd be surprised what people have to say. "One reference check we completed for a new contractor ended with a wish of 'Good luck,' with an implied, 'you'll need it.' We assigned work anyway, and that contractor proved to be a challenge for us," says former personal concierge and guide author Jennifer James.

- Develop a training manual before you hire. If you want to keep your methods confidential, don't send the manual home, but have the employee study it on the job. To develop your training manual, keep notes as you complete tasks for clients, so you can pass these details along to your employees.

- Train your employees to keep careful records of time spent, as you'll need this to bill your clients. Provide them with your tracking forms, or use a system where they phone in as they arrive at or leave a client's home.

- Develop a "nose" for sensing the kinds of tasks that are best delegated, and those that are better done yourself. The client and his or her tastes may factor into your decision as well.

5.5   On-the-Job Strategies

Chapter 2 explains many of the tasks a personal concierge may take on, and how to complete them. But how you put your day together with these tasks and how you handle the unexpected will have a major impact on the success of your business.

5.5.1   Managing Your Time Effectively

As a personal concierge, you give people the gift of time. In order to do this and run a successful business, you have to be constantly looking for ways to be more efficient than the average person.

The first step in managing your time effectively is to determine what hours you want to work. Not only how many hours, but in what range you want or need those hours to fall. So if you have to pick your children up from school at 3:30 and the bus picks them up by 7:30, then your standard work hours may be 8 a.m. to 3 p.m. daily, Monday to Friday.

Setting specified working hours can sometimes be difficult since a personal concierge is often expected to be available at the drop of a hat. "As the owner of a concierge company, " Dustyn Shroff notes, "you have to be ready, willing and able to pick up the phone, check your email, and conduct normal operations at any time of day or night."

If you don't set specified hours and communicate them to your clients, they are likely to call any time of the day or night. "Setting a good pace and not overburdening yourself will allow you to provide top-notch customer service, which is key in this business," explains Delmar Johnson of The Concierge Place.

If you simplify the task-request process for clients, you'll spend less time interacting with clients, and more time getting things done. It's not that you want to avoid your clients, but they are time-starved and probably want to streamline how they request services. Make it easy to contact you by phone, text message, or email. Or you can limit person-to-person requests by having other ways for clients to communicate with you.

If you create a system where they are less likely to forget things they want to ask you about, you help cut back on panicked phone calls that cause you to drop everything and meet a need. For example, if you designate a "concierge message center" in the client's home, you'll know exactly where to look for information about what is needed from you that day. Anticipating needs or suggesting services they may not have thought of also cuts down on last-minute emergencies down the road.

Agree on protocols: dirty clothing in the blue basket is ready to go to the dry cleaners. An empty box of highlighters left in a certain place signifies that the client would like you to purchase a replacement. Last week's menu with dishes crossed out or circled indicates that they did or did not go over well with the family.

More Time-Management Strategies

- Assess clients' needs as they come in, and prioritize accordingly. Find out real deadlines — don't settle for ASAP since every need will be preferred ASAP. Ask questions until you have a real handle on the situation.

- Know that time you shave off running errands is money back in your pocket — so long as saving time isn't at a cost to you. For example, getting a parking ticket while you try to quickly run an errand cuts into your profit margin beyond any time you saved looking for legal parking. You can save time by planning out a route in advance.

- Expect that certain times of the year like the Christmas season will be busier, and plan accordingly. Maybe you'll need some temporary help around that time. To avoid burnout, limit the number of hours you work in a day.

- Have a backup plan in case you get sick or have an emergency. Put this in your contract.

- Consider having some rainy-day projects in the wings that you can work on if your client needs to cancel a scheduled service. These can be projects of your own, or specific projects for your client that allow you to bill for those hours.

- Concierge Jill Burstein says that one of the biggest mistakes she sees others in the business make is that they don't get around to answering their emails. Not getting back immediately to the potential client is a great way to lose business!

- If you don't have a specific amount of time booked with a client, let them know when you arrive how much time you have for them that day. If there are unresolved issues, schedule a follow-up appointment for as soon as possible.

- Use networking opportunities to develop an "emergency network" of other personal concierges or similar service providers you can turn to for advice. A quick answer from a colleague can save hours of research or failed attempts to solve a problem. And learn to recognize when it's time to call in a contractor instead.

Keep yourself organized too. Use a PDA or a good planning system. Take a lot of notes. Make time in your week for administrative tasks, such as updating client files. Keep your bookkeeping up to date with a program like QuickBooks, so it's not a daunting task that you put off from week to week.

"I hate the clerical part of running a business," confesses personal concierge Jill Burstein. "I am a creative, 'ideas' person who is running a business that I am passionate about. I like talking to clients and potential clients. I like running around. I don't like numbers and reports and Excel spreadsheets and the like. Yuck. So I am hunting down help in the form of an assistant and a few errand runners to fill in my gaps."

5.5.2   Handling the Unexpected

As a personal concierge, you won't always be in or near your office when the need for an item or supply strikes. Always have your list of preferred vendors and contact information on you so you can respond quickly, stored either in your PDA or paper organizer. A laptop computer can also be an invaluable asset to the personal concierge.

When you head out to clients, have accurate directions to where you need to go, and contact information for the client in case you get lost. A map or GPS is an essential in-car supply. You can also pack an on-the-go supply box for your car that includes some or all of the following items:

- A few pens, a Sharpie and a highlighter
- Aspirin
- Bag of plastic gloves
- Cheap camera
- Comfortable walking shoes
- Container of various nails and screws
- Emergency numbers
- Extra nylons, socks, and/or necktie
- First-aid kit
- Flashlight
- Hammer

- Kleenex
- Multi-tool
- Non-perishable snacks and a few bottles of water
- Notepad
- Plastic garbage bags
- Pack of CD-ROMs
- Paper towels
- Scarf, hat, gloves, umbrella
- Screwdrivers (various heads and sizes)
- Spot/stain remover
- Stamps
- Tape measure
- Two changes of clothing (professional and casual)
- Wet wipes

Impress your clients (and make your life easier) by being prepared for anything that comes your way.

A Note on Personal Safety

As a personal concierge, you need to keep your own safety and security forefront in your mind. Meet new clients first in a public place, or bring along an assistant for initial meetings. Let someone know where you're going to be, and when you expect to return. If a client makes you uncomfortable in any way, leave immediately, and don't go back.

Beyond personal safety, you also have to be mindful of unusual requests and odd situations. Identity theft is a hot issue these days — ensure that credit card numbers provided by clients over the phone are their own. Don't get roped into an illegal act by not keeping your senses on red alert, especially with clients who want to do business quickly and without personal contact.

6. Getting Personal Concierge Clients

6.1 Your Marketing Plan

Your marketing plan will lay the groundwork of how you plan to attract a base of clients for your business. Your plan should be within your budget, and it should also be measurable. You need to know that the money or effort you put out is working for you. Here are some considerations in developing a unique marketing plan for your business.

6.1.1 Evaluating the Market

To evaluate whether your local market can support a personal concierge business, you can look at some demographic data for your region. Contact community associations, town halls, the courthouse, the city, or whoever keeps data on the local population. You want to look for trends that denote your typical client: two-income families, high income levels, etc. For more about finding and using demographic data, see section 3.5.2.

Look also to data that would support a particular specialization: a higher-than-average birth rate (coupled with above-average family income) might indicate that a service specializing in helping new mothers after childbirth would be welcomed. A larger senior population would suggest targeting that market with services geared toward senior care.

> *"Many of my clients have mobility or health issues, or are really busy. None of them is rich and wants somebody to help spend their millions."*
>
> — Jill Burstein,
>   personal concierge in the Detroit area

Even if the data that comes back is generally unsupportive, take heart. Personal concierge businesses are somewhat unique in that you don't need large numbers of clients to be busy full time. Anywhere from 10 to 40 clients is typical in this industry. You only need as many clients as will keep you busy for the number of hours you want to work.

For example, eight clients who need you for five hours a week generates forty hours of business. On the other hand, five clients who need you for eight hours generate the same. The fewer the clients you cater to, the more personalized service you will be able to provide for them. Knowing them well helps you retain clients, and generate additional income by suggesting services.

Evaluating the Competition

As mentioned earlier, it's always a good idea to determine who your competitors are. There may be 20 personal concierge businesses operating in a 50-mile radius of you, or there may be none. The first scenario certainly makes it easier to evaluate the competition and general market for your services, but there are also ways to test uncharted waters. As mentioned in section 5.2, Setting Your Fees, you can study businesses operating in similar market conditions to yours.

When you study the competition or similar businesses, take a look at what services these concierges are offering. Do they specialize in any way? What categories do they break services into? What do they charge? What marketing messages are they using? Make a chart to compare several examples, and look for trends. (See section 3.5.2 for a sample chart you can use to compare the strengths and weaknesses of your competitors.)

If everyone seems to have the same type of business or specialization, you may want to go a different direction. Is there a portion of the market that is currently under-served? Think "different," but be aware that straying too far from what clients already use can negatively affect the marketability of your work.

Another way to look at it is that, if the market is currently supporting a certain type of business, then you know the client base exists. You can chip away a share of that business for yourself by offering better service, or a better price. Don't assume that just because it's not being done, there's no market for it. But on the other hand, don't assume that because there is already a lot of competition that you won't thrive.

6.1.2   Finding a Niche

Finding a niche means identifying a way to make your services stand out from the competition. Some ways you can do this are by targeting a distinct client base, or by varying your service level or pricing structure. You can also specialize in a certain service or group of services, as section 6.1.3 will explain.

Your niche can be as specialized or unique as your local market will support. Something related to your local market may even be in order, such as boaters, vacationers, or tourists. If you have worked in other industries before (medical or legal services, for example) and have inside knowledge of them, you can turn your familiarity into a selling point for your service.

Some common market specializations in this industry include the following. You can think about your local market, your background, and what might make sense for your business:

- New entrepreneurs
- Senior services
- Vacationers

- New mother help

- Convalescents

- Big or busy families

- Single men

- Traveling business people

- Members of an exclusive club

- Employees of a single employer

- People who work in a certain industry (e.g., doctors)

- Residents of a particular neighborhood (even if it isn't yours)

- Only men or women

- University professors

- Small business owners

- Celebrities or the extremely wealthy

In the personal concierge industry, it seems logical to think that you are a jack-of-all-trades, and that specializing in a certain service, geographic area, or type of client will only limit your client base. While this is certainly true, you do need to limit your services, even at the outset, to a simple subgroup of the population: those who can both pay for them and have a need for them.

If you think you will have trouble choosing a specialization off the top, approach it in this way. Think about your "perfect client," as in the people you would most enjoy working with. Are they male or female? What is their job? Do they have kids or pets? Do they live near you? What is their income level? Describe their personality: business-like, friendly, chatty, professional, distant?

Once you have your ideal client in mind, target your marketing to this client. When you land a client that fits this profile, focus your energy on them. Suggest additional ways you can be of service, and ask for referrals to their friends (who are most likely to be like your ideal client). You'll still service other clients, but pursue their business less vigorously. Over time this will prune your client base into exactly what you envision.

Personal concierge Elyse Coleman who runs Life/Time CEO shares this story about how she has refined her specialized services to be more personal than most:

> "One of my clients called me at 9 o'clock on a Sunday evening asking if I knew someone she could call to stay with her that evening. She was alone in her apartment and was feeling a little vulnerable. In that instance, I knew her situation well enough that I was able to address her concerns by reviewing with her all the security measures she had in place, and [reminding her] that an aide would be there the next morning at 7 a.m.

> "I see this as an example of good listening skills, and having the ability to address a client's *real need* rather than just fulfilling her initial request. That is the kind of service that I believe sets one apart as a provider of lifestyle services, as opposed to being an errand service. Some concierge services are designed to function at the errand level, and others such as Life/Time CEO are at the other end of the spectrum."

6.1.3   Choosing Services to Offer

Before you launch your business, you'll need to develop a list of services you offer, commonly referred to as a services menu. The idea is that clients can order off the menu, as well as requesting special services when needed. You choose whether or not to meet the special request. Too many services can be overwhelming, so focus on some core services you know are needed. Once you get a foot in the door, you can suggest other ways you can be of service.

Do Your Homework

To help identify core services, start by making a list of the tasks you yourself currently are putting off. Ask friends, family, and colleagues: "If you had a day off to get up to five things done, what would you do with your day?" The tasks that come up time and time again are the services you'll want to focus on and promote. You can do similar research with a survey conducted in a mall in the area you want to target.

If you have a target market in mind, think about the services they are most likely to need. What limitations besides time do they experience? You can refer back to the subsections in Chapter 2, each of which touch on services you may offer or specialize in.

Chances are you will offer at least grocery shopping, errand running, and organizing, and expand from there based on your interests, skills, and market. For example, Bev Riggins of Midwest Concierge Service says that in her area, house-sitting and organizational assistance are the services the general public has the greatest need for. Jill Burstein in Detroit identified grocery shopping, gift shopping and car maintenance, and added dry cleaning pick-up and drop-off.

"I believe the top-three concierge services would fall into the categories of organizational services (people are disorganized in their homes and offices and seek help in de-cluttering); household services that could include waiting for a repairman or house sitting when on vacation or long trips; and finally, errand services — particularly grocery shopping," says Delmar Johnson.

Two Specialization Options

One business model seeing success right now is the online concierge service. These concierges work with tenants of office buildings or condos, and provide services that can be ordered or executed online, such as obtaining sports, theater and movie tickets, ordering flowers, or booking travel. Clients simply log on to the website to order services. (You can read about Eservus, one of these online concierges, at **www.eservusconcierge.com/online/index.asp**).

Virtual assistants operate in a similar way, taking on administrative, creative or technical assignments by email, and doing any task that doesn't require them to be in the client's office. For example, filing would be a no-go, but writing and editing services or website maintenance would be good offerings. Your clients can be down the road or around the world, and payment is easy to arrange with PayPal. You can visit the International Virtual Assistants Association at **www.ivaa.org** to learn more about this service, which is essentially a very specialized branch of what personal concierges do.

Exclusions

Part of your service planning will also include determining if there are any services you will not offer. "I exclude travel arrangements and party planning at this point," says Jill Burstein of Jill will... Concierge Service. "I think that travel is best left up to the professionals, as liability concerns and all the details just complicate things tremendously. And I love helping for a party, i.e. setting up, running errands and even brainstorming for decor and such; but I don't have the experience in putting the whole shebang together.

"Also, I don't typically stay overnight when house-sitting, but on a rare occasion, I wouldn't refuse if needed. Otherwise, I am pretty open. But I will tell people that something is out of my scope if I am not 100 percent sure I can do something to the highest standards," she points out.

6.2 Marketing Tools

Your marketing tools serve an important role. They speak for your business 24 hours a day — they are your representative when you are not there to talk about your work. These tools remind past clients of your services, and let potential clients learn more about what you do. They should be matched to your target market in wording, image selection, and quality.

6.2.1 Your Website

Today's consumers expect you to have a web presence, and will often decide not to do business with you if you neglect this aspect of your marketing. While the idea of creating a website may seem intimidating, it doesn't have to be complicated.

What to Include

The focus of the site should be the services you provide or specialize in, and the benefits for the client. Your website can include any of the following:

- Home page with links to navigate through your site. Your home page may also include some of the items listed below.

- "About Us" page so that your customers can learn more about you and your company. This should include your credentials and a photograph of you.

- Where you work out of and where you are willing to travel to.

- Testimonial quotes from satisfied clients.

- Information about your prices and packages, including any current promotions.

- Helpful information you have written such as tips on how to find more time in your day, tips on getting organized, and other content that shows your expertise. Adding new content on a regular basis can keep people returning to your site.

- FAQ (Frequently Asked Questions) with answers so you can save time during consultations.

- A way to send you a message or contact you immediately. Your company name, telephone number and email address should ideally be on every page, but you can also have a "Contact Us" page with your contact information.

- Additional items could include your privacy policy, any products for sale, a sign-up for your newsletter, and your brochure (see section 6.2.2.) as a PDF.

TIP: As a member of a very young industry, part of your marketing will be educating people about what you do. Don't forget to include a component of education about personal concierges and concierge services on your website and in your brochures.

You can get ideas of what to include on your own website by visiting sites of other personal concierge businesses. (See the links provided throughout this book.)

Designing Your Website

Software such as Adobe Dreamweaver has made the creation of web pages possible for everyone. However, one problem with creating and maintaining a website on your own is that it can be time-consuming to build and to keep up-to-date. If you don't have the time to spend on creating a polished website, you may prefer to have a professional web designer build and maintain your site. There is no shortage of web designers, so consult your local phone directory or search online for one in your area.

Images conveying family time, relaxation, or organization can be very effective. If you don't mind paying extra to a web designer, a slideshow of images set to music or a short video, especially as an intro, can be eye-catching as well.

Special Features

In vogue right now is the blog or "weblog," an online diary where you share more of yourself and your day-to-day business. You can't blog in a way that compromises your clients' privacy, but you can talk about the industry in general and your passion for what you do. Blogger.com makes it easy for you to set up a blog and link to it from your site. To be effective, blogs need to be updated frequently — at least once a week.

Another complementary feature to a website is an e-newsletter. As you collect email addresses from clients, you add them (with their permission only) into your database of contacts. You can then send a newsletter that talks about current promotions, offers discounts, and showcases press you've received or changes you've made to the business. You can also give clients tips to find more time or live better. Your newsletters, after distribution, can be archived online. You can send out e-newsletters inexpensively through a company such as Constant Contact at **www.constant contact.com**. The cost is based on the size of your email list, starting at $15 per month for a list of up to 500 people, and a free trial is available.

Hosting and Domain Names

Once your web pages are prepared you will need to find an Internet service provider (ISP) server to host them. Many web designers are also in the business of hosting, as are those who register domain names. While the company you use to connect to the Internet may offer free web pages, you should use a hosting company that will allow you to use your own domain name, such as www.yourbusinessname.com.

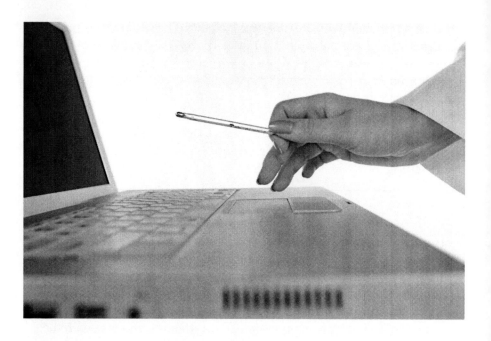

When choosing a domain name it's best to use your business name or something closely resembling it. One popular site where you can search for and register your domain name is GoDaddy.com. They also offer inexpensive web hosting services. Visit **www.godaddy.com** to find out more.

Getting It Out There

> *It's no secret that the first place people turn to is the internet when they need something they can't find at the local grocery/convenience store. Making your name and your brand visible on the world wide web is essential to your success! It's not cheap, but invest money in it if you can — gain the recognition you not only need but deserve. You may have a fantastic product, but if nobody knows about it, then they'll never use it!"*

— Dustyn Shroff, One Concierge

No matter how much you spend on your website, if people don't know it exists, it won't help your business. Make certain you list your site on all your business forms, cards, and brochures.

To help people find your website you'll want to submit it to the search engines, and possibly include a list of key words somewhere inconspicuous to help locate your service. You can also submit your website to online directories, such as the ones listed below. Local and state service directories as well as travel directories may also be helpful to land new clients.

- *Business.com: Concierge Services*
  www.business.com/general/concierge-services

- *Canadian Concierge Directory*
  http://canadianconciergedirectory.com

- *Yahoo: Concierge Services*
  http://dir.yahoo.com/Business_and_Economy/Business_to_Business/Hospitality_Industry/Concierge_Services

Your website can be an important tool for marketing your services. It gives your prospects an opportunity to learn more about you and your services at their convenience. It may also expose you to a potentially unlimited audience of those in need of your services.

6.2.2 Printed Materials

Your printed materials include business cards, stationery (such as letterhead, envelopes, and mailing labels), and other marketing materials such as brochures.

If you have a computer with a high quality laser or ink jet printer, you may be able to inexpensively print professional looking materials from your own computer. Free templates for all the print materials you are likely to need in your business can be found online.

HP offers templates for use in a variety of programs at **www.hp.com/sbso/productivity/office**. For example, you can create a matching set of stationery (business cards, letterhead, envelopes) in Microsoft Word. The site includes free online classes and how-to guides to help you design your own marketing materials.

Another excellent resource is the Microsoft Office Online Templates Homepage at **http://office.microsoft.com/en-us/templates**. At this site you can search a database to find templates for:

- Business stationery (envelopes, faxes, labels, letters, memos, etc.)

- Marketing materials (brochures, flyers, newsletters, postcards, etc.)

- Meeting documents (agendas, minutes, presentations, slides, etc.)

- Other business documents (expense reports, invoices, receipts, time sheets, etc.)

As an alternative to printing materials yourself, and for materials that won't fit through your printer (such as folders), consider using a company that provides printing services. Your printed materials can be easily designed, paid for and delivered without leaving the house. Here are links to some companies that provide printing services for small businesses:

- *FedEx Office*
  www.fedex.com/us/office/online-printing-services.html

- *Acecomp Plus – Printing Solutions*
  www.acecomp.com/printing.asp

- *The Paper Mill Store*
  www.thepapermillstore.com

- *VistaPrint*
  www.vistaprint.com

While the resources listed above can help with all your printing needs, here is some advice about two types of materials that are particularly important for marketing purposes – business cards and brochures.

Business Cards

Business cards should state your name, your business name, your phone number, your email address, and your website. You can list your home address as your business location, but most people who work from home choose to leave this detail out. This prevents anyone from bothering you after hours, or losing business because people think you are area-specific.

Your business card should be printed on good-quality card stock, in a font that reads clearly. In this very personal business, a photo of you is not out of place on your card. You should be able to get several hundred business cards printed for less than $100. Expect to pay a bit more for gloss or four-color printing when you include a photo.

If your budget is limited, a good source for high quality low-cost cards (currently $19.99 per 250 cards) is VistaPrint at **www.vistaprint.com**. Visit their site to see a wide variety of designs you can consider.

Brochures

Brochures come in handy when you are targeting corporate clients, or are not able to arrange a face-to-face meeting right away. A brochure can also be left with service providers such as high-end spas and hotels, or distributed by mail or by hand to targeted client bases.

If you decide to create a brochure for your business, here are items you can include:

- Your company name

- Contact information

- Your web address

- A description of your professional qualifications

- A description of the benefit of your services

- Information about the services you provide

- A photograph of you

- Testimonial quotes from satisfied clients

Often misunderstood, the purpose of a brochure is not to land business, but to pique interest. You don't need to cover every service you provide, but emphasize the benefits for clients who use your service: more time with family, less stress, more time for hobbies, less frustration, etc. Let them know you will be quick, professional, and discreet.

Focus on the fact that you can save people time and money. Time for obvious reasons, and also money because your efforts make them more efficient, and they don't overpay for items or services because they are rushed.

Match the quality of your brochure to the cost of your service. If you are printing only a few copies of your brochure, you may be able to find nice paper at your local office supply store or one of the websites listed earlier in this section, which you can run through your printer. If you have brochures professionally printed, the cost may be a few hundred dollars (for one color on simple cardstock).

Many printers will have an in-house design department who can do the artwork for you, but you are traditionally expected to supply the copy (i.e. the words). And why not? You are the best-qualified person to describe what you can do for a client.

The wording you use on your website often translates well to a brochure. Get the two written at once to save time and cost, or use one set of great copy on both.

Finally, personal concierge Jill Burstein makes an important and often-overlooked point: "Don't make simple spelling mistakes on your website and marketing materials because you didn't have a professional proofread it, or bother to use spell-check. *'We can due anything you need done. Were their for you.'* That spells 'amateur,' or that you just don't care or are very sloppy," she says.

6.2.3   Advertisements

You'll hear a lot of people tell you that advertising doesn't work, and in some cases that's true. Ads need to be designed to catch your clients' attention, and pique their interest in some way. Timing, placement in a publication, and how many times you are willing to run the ad can make a big difference in the way your ad is received.

Yellow Pages

You have probably used the Yellow Pages many times. But before you buy an ad for your own business, you should carefully investigate the costs compared to the potential return. Many new business owners find a Yellow Pages ad does not make the phone ring off the hook with buyers. If someone does respond to your ad, they may be "shopping around," so you must be prepared to invest time as well as advertising dollars if you use this method of advertising.

To minimize your risk, you might want to consider starting with a small display ad, such as a 1/8 page ad. If you can get your hands on a previous year's edition of your local Yellow Pages, compare the ads from year to year. Look for categories such as "concierge services" or "personal services." If you notice others have increased or decreased the size of their ads, this can give you an indication of what might work for you. Also, if you are doing information interviews, you can ask personal concierges how well their Yellow Pages ads are working for them.

You can either design the ad yourself, have the Yellow Pages design it for you, or hire a designer. Take a look at the ads in the events category of your current Yellow Pages for ideas. If you are interested in advertising, contact your local Yellow Pages to speak with a sales rep. Check your phone book for contact information. See the suggestions below for tips on what to include in your ad.

> **TIP:** Some localities also have "pages" or "books" of other types. In the mid-Atlantic states, the community Yellow Pages are alternatives. These are limited to smaller geographic areas than, for example, a whole state or city. Check into that possibility, as well, especially if you don't want to travel great distances to find clients.

Magazines and Newspapers

Magazine and newspaper advertising is most effective when it is targeted. You can take out an ad in a publication that doesn't reach your target market, and get no results. Alternately you can spend some money advertising in a format that reaches people who have a need for your services, and get a return rate that more than justifies the cost.

This type of advertising can be expensive, and may not generate the results you want unless you do it repeatedly. (It has been estimated that people need to see an advertisement three to seven times before buying.)

If you choose to buy advertising, it will probably be most cost-effective to place ads in small local magazines or newspapers. The publications you advertise in will usually design your ad for an additional cost, and give you a copy of the ad to run in other publications. Here are some tips for effective advertising:

- Make your ad about your customers. Explain how they can benefit from your services rather than just listing the services you provide.

- Make them an offer they can't refuse. Advertising generates more results when there is a reason for the reader to act. Consider offering a discount to first-time clients (10 or 20 percent), or an hour of service for free. Offers should be for a limited time only, and subject to certain conditions. Say "call today" and have an expiry date for your offer.

- Make sure you're available for people who respond to your ad. If someone wants to talk to you but keeps getting your voice mail, they may give up.

- Make long-term plans for your advertising program. Chances are that running an ad once won't give you as much business as you would hope.

You should always know if your advertising is working for you, or you're just throwing money into the wind. Try to find a way to track how clients found you, by using a coupon code for example, or asking them when they call. Have measurable goals for the advertising you pay for, and if the money doesn't come back to you, don't go that route again.

Other Options

There's no one single way to reach potential clients, since every personal concierge business is different. In addition to magazines and newspapers that your target market reads, here are some alternative options you may wish to try out:

- Door hangers in high-end neighborhoods

- Craigslist (**www.craigslist.org**)

- School newsletters

- Community or condo association publications

"I use pink signs on my kooky car," says personal concierge Jill Burstein, talking about what marketing tools have worked best for her so far. "I have had people chasing me down and having me pull over to talk to me, and others making their kids write down my phone number as they pull up to the light. They've netted me a few great clients. And I wear my name and number on my back while I work — embroidery is cheap and effective," she notes.

6.3   Getting Positive Publicity

Publicity for your business is great because it gets your name out there at a low cost or for free. When newspapers or magazines write about you, clients are more likely to notice and trust that information than what they see in an ad, which they know is paid for. When you donate to charities, people associate you with goodwill and the community. And when you position yourself as an expert, clients build trust in your services.

6.3.1   Write a Press Release

Press releases are short notices you send to the media (print, TV, radio, and online) to generate interest in your business. Whenever you do something newsworthy, it's time to send out a press release so clients hear about it. You can write press releases about things that have happened as well as about things that are going to happen. Be sure to send a press release when you:

- First start up your business

- Expand your services

- Sponsor an event or contest

- Make a charitable donation

Because personal concierge services are such a new concept, they are often newsworthy in themselves. Therefore you can also send out timely press releases about work/family balance issues, as well as the ways that personal concierges factor into today's lifestyles.

When you send out a press release, you should have available on request your bio and a professional-quality photo of yourself, some FAQ (frequently asked questions) about the profession, clients who are willing to be contacted about your service, a few unusual requests or colorful stories, and some other news clips about the profession. These can become part of your press kit, which you can use to land interviews with media such as TV and radio.

Like your advertising, your press releases should be sent to targeted media. Most magazines and newspapers publish contact information for their editors. Newspapers may have dozens of editors, so make sure you send your submission to the appropriate one.

Format

Editors prefer to see a press release as a single page (fewer than 500 words), and written as if it were a news story. A press release may be printed verbatim if the editor is willing, or it may be revised.

Here are some general guidelines for writing a press release:

- Make sure the press release is newsworthy. For example, you could write about a new industry trend or a type of service request you are seeing gain popularity.

- Give your press release a strong lead paragraph that answers the six main questions: who, what, where, when, why, and how.

- Include your contact information at the end of the press release so reporters can get in touch with you.

As a personal concierge, your best skills may not lie in writing. You can hire a freelance writer or PR professional to write press releases for you, and possibly to track and/or follow up on them. To keep your outlay of cash down, see if they would be willing to trade their services for yours. Otherwise, you can find numerous online resources to help you write a press release, including:

- *How to Write a Great Press Release: A Sample Press Release Template*
  www.publicityinsider.com/release.asp

- *PRWeb: Writing Great Online News Releases*
  **http://service.prweb.com/pr/_assets/downloads/
  how-to-write-press-releases.pdf**

On the next page is a sample press release you can use. Add your own information in place of the italicized words, and revise it as needed to include your own comments and examples.

Sample Press Release

LOCAL BUSINESS SELLS TIME TO BUSY PEOPLE AND FAMILIES

Today's Date

For Immediate Release

(Your Town, State) — *Business Name,* a new business in *Your Town,* has starting offering a valuable and innovative service to local individuals and businesses: they will do the things on your to-do list, so that you have more free time in your day. Called "personal concierges," *Your Business'* team of errand runners are can-do specialists who are reliable, discreet, and can handle any assignment, from grocery shopping, to gift buying, to taking the dog to the groomers.

There's never been a better time for time-saving services in *Your Town,* as the time crisis in North America has reached new heights, and the challenges of balancing family and work are taking their toll. The Families and Work Institute reports that more than half of U.S. employees surveyed felt "overworked at least sometimes" in the last three months. In response, the International Concierge and Errand Association estimates that personal concierge services have now become a $1 billion industry worldwide.

Your Name, owner of *Business Name,* recognized that every person's time is precious, and decided to open a business that gives people back the gift of time in their busy lives. "Why spend time waiting in line at the grocery store when you can be at your son's soccer game, taking your significant other out for dinner, or just relaxing at home for a change?" he/she points out. "Our clients range from businesses who want to reward or attract employees, to dual-income families, to busy professionals. Everyone could use a little more free time in their lives."

Business Name's many clients agree that relief from time-consuming tasks like getting the car serviced, waiting for contactors to arrive, or buying gifts is a welcome service. *"Insert a quote here from a satisfied client, who states the benefits your service provides."*

Your Business opened in *Your Town* in *Year,* with a mission to *(state your unique vision or mission).* Their concierge services include *(list of your services or specialties).* More information about the company is available at *Your Website.*

Contact: Your Name, owner, Business Name
                Your Phone Number(s)
                Your Website

6.3.2   Donations and Sponsorships

Donations and sponsorships are a good way to raise awareness of your business without a substantial cost, since your only contribution is your time. They are also a good route to target the wealthy, who are often involved with philanthropic causes. The added benefit is that money is raised for worthy causes that help out people in need.

To take part in silent auctions or other events, you'll need to have gift certificates printed up, and create a small display that promotes your involvement. Gift certificates are best if they are transferable, so the client can re-gift it if desired. Include a brochure with the gift certificate so the recipient gets an idea of what you do.

Your display should be appropriate to the audience, eye-catching, and convey somehow what you do. A collage of pictures of people relaxing and enjoying their free time could be done nicely, or you could incorporate a classy-looking clock that draws people over. If you volunteer your time to work at an event, you can talk to people on site about what you do.

Your services as a personal concierge are also a useful bartering tool to encourage awareness of your business. A free block of time (4-6 hours) makes great prize for a radio station to offer, and your business gets the on-air mention (free advertising). Select only the radio stations that can show you that their listener demographic is your target market, though.

While it's important to give something back, remember that there is still a real cost to you in donating your time. You can keep a running total of your charitable donations in terms of what you would have charged, and when you hit a significant milestone, send out a press release announcing your achievement.

6.3.3   Be Seen As an Expert

As a personal concierge, you have a unique career that people are almost always interested in hearing about. People will ask you for advice on how to organize their closets or figure out their newest technology gadget. When you make yourself available as a teacher or mentor, you reinforce your image as an expert in your field. And that's good for business.

Start by becoming a visible part of your community. If you target families with hyper-scheduled children, join community associations (take a board position), the parent-teacher association, and other groups that take an interest in children's wellbeing. Volunteer to speak to local seniors about strategies for downsizing their living accommodations, and don't leave out the fact that you can help them pack and relocate.

In addition to press releases, you can submit articles to local publications on topics that relate to your expertise. If you are talented at writing, you can pitch the editor on a weekly or monthly column dealing with different aspects of work/life balance, or managing a household. If you get enough articles together, you can self-publish them as a tip book, and provide this book free of charge via your website. Again, if writing is not your thing, you can arrange for a ghostwriter to draft something up for you based on information you provide.

Offering to teach seminars or workshops is also a great way to meet prospective clients. Don't worry about giving away your trade secrets —

people will still have little time to implement your ideas themselves. Most people just want to learn how to get a bit more organized, and making a personal connection is effective in landing clients. Contact the continuing education department of your local college if you have an idea for a course.

You can also phone local radio and TV shows and let them know that you are available to comment on work/life balance issues, or give advice to people looking to find some more free time or get organized. Shows that might be appropriate include morning shows and afternoon talk shows, where the content tends to be lighter. Your contact should be the producer of the show.

6.4   Referrals and Word-of-Mouth Business

Personal concierges will tell you that referrals and word of mouth are their main sources of new business. Here are some ways to create word-of-mouth buzz by building relationships with clients, their families, and other service providers.

6.4.1   From Other Businesses

Arranging strategic partnerships with other personal service providers is a very effective way to win referrals. Think of personal shoppers, personal chefs, limousine drivers, butlers, personal trainers, housekeepers, florists, consultants, party planners, agents or managers, nannies, real estate agents, and executive assistants — they all have contact with your potential clients.

At some point, client requests are likely to exceed these other individuals' boundaries of service. An executive assistant doesn't necessarily have the connections or know-how to plan a romantic dinner to surprise his boss' fiancée. But if he knows enough to call you to arrange it, the problem is solved. Similarly, a housekeeper may not be able to wait around for the furnace repair person to arrive, so she refers her client to you instead.

To help build positive, win-win relationships with other service providers, start by referring (or offering to refer) your clients to them when you get requests for services that are beyond your scope of expertise.

You can arrange partnerships with service providers that give their clients a discount on your services, and vice-versa.

A partnership arrangement with a local high-end clothing store where clients who spend $1,000 or more get a gift certificate for a free block of time could be profitable for you, since you are targeting people who clearly have money to spend. These incentives benefit the store as well, since they add value to what they can offer their clients.

Although it may seem like a strange idea at first, other personal concierges can be a great source of referral business. Concierges working on their own cannot be in two places at once. Especially come the holiday season, the chances that the other concierges are already run off their feet are quite high. Having a backup person to call can be a great relief. Build relationships with other concierges at networking events, or by contacting them directly. And be sure to return the favor when you can.

One Concierge CEO Dustyn Shroff advises, "the concierge industry is one that is made up of only individuals who want to help one another. Assisting clients is a priority in any industry," he continues, "but with us, assisting each other is also key."

Meet up with other service professionals by joining service clubs or by taking part in a local chapter of an organization dedicated to networking and mutual referrals, such as Business Network International (**www.bni.com**). Networking clubs are covered in detail in section 6.5.1.

It's important to say thank you to each and every business contact who refers you, not just the first time but every time they do so. A handwritten note is often appropriate, and in some cases a small gift basket is better. If someone is in the position to refer you often, you may want to take them out to lunch for a personal meeting. Just don't set the bar too high right away, or you'll go broke trying to keep up with your thank-yous.

6.4.2   From Satisfied Clients

The best ways to generate word-of-mouth business from your existing or past clients are to do great work, and offer exceptional service. Make sure clients are always 100% satisfied, and they will start telling people about you.

So, what is exceptional service? Generally, it's going beyond what the client has asked for to add little thoughtful touches, or meeting their needs before they are spoken. Do it faster, save them money, and add value where you can. Specifically, it's anything you can think of that will give your client the "wow" feeling about your work. If there are ever any problems, they are dealt with swiftly without any further inconvenience to the client.

"We will personalize to suit the company or the individual," explains Jill Burstein about her company, Jill will... Concierge Service. "I don't mind changing my typical routine if it suits my client better. If they need something very early or very late, we take care of it even if the contract states specific hours. I like making sure they are taken care of, and they are very appreciative."

If you want to know how your service ranks with clients, you have to ask. Don't assume because you hear nothing that everything was perfect — there's always room for improvement. Work methods of evaluation into your way of doing business, and ask for client feedback often.

You'll have to walk a fine line to get people who are time-starved to take the time to respond to something like a written questionnaire, so maybe you can add an incentive such as a draw for 10 hours of your time, or a free Spring Clean-Up Package.

You can use similar incentives to get your clients to refer you to their friends. The first step is simply to ask for referrals. Clients may assume you have all the clients you need, but if you ask them to refer their friends to you, they will have that in the backs of their minds. Give them extra copies of your business cards to make referrals a breeze. You can also give coupons to your best clients for four free hours of service, which they can give as gifts to friends. That gives the friend an immediate reason to pick up the phone and call you.

6.4.3　Testimonials

Testimonials are a great way to let potential clients get an idea of the quality of your service before you even meet them. Included on your website or in a brochure, they will offer people unfamiliar with you and your company to read the words of other satisfied clients. Like word of mouth referrals, they're a recommendation of you that help others make up their minds about enlisting the services of your company.

Testimonial Letters

One type of testimonial is the testimonial letter. This is essentially a letter of reference from someone who has used your services and it can help you land additional clients. If your client is particularly happy with the services you have provided, don't be afraid to ask them for a letter.

When you ask a client for a testimonial letter, be sure that they provide an outstanding review of you and your services. A mediocre letter can actually hurt your chances of getting hired. A mediocre letter reflects a mediocre service provider and who would want to hire a mediocre personal concierge?

Most of your clients will be busy people and may simply not have the desire to take the time to sit down and think of great words to applaud your services. Instead of putting this kind of pressure on them, simply write up a glowing letter yourself and review it with the client. If they're happy with what you've written, have them sign it and you've got a great testimonial letter from a satisfied client. Be sure you mention to your client that you'd like to use it in your marketing materials to ensure they're okay with it.

Questionnaires

Another way to get a testimonial is to follow up at the end of the service contract with a client with a questionnaire. This will give you feedback about what they did or did not like about your services and allow you to adjust your service delivery appropriately. At the same time, you can use any positive comments you receive as a testimonial to the quality of your services. Again, check with clients to see that they're okay with you using their names in your marketing materials. You can use their comments anonymously, but anonymous testimonials don't carry the same weight. People can easily assume that you made it up.

6.5 Selling Your Services

Marketing and promoting your business with ads or press releases is not the same thing as "selling." Selling is something that is done person-to-person, and occurs after someone has an awareness of your service, but is not sure that you have anything to offer them personally. Marketing can't work unless you have good sales skills to close the deal. This section deals with meeting people face to face and selling what you can do for them.

6.5.1   Networking

When you first start your personal concierge business, you will be focused on landing clients. You may start with one or two clients already, or you may jump right in with none. Either way, you will be making daily efforts early on in your career to meet potential clients and convince them of the value of your service. (Once you are more established, you can usually lay off the aggressive tactics, although you'll still want to maintain the connections you established.)

Start with the people you know, often referred to as your "warm contacts." Let immediate family and friends know what you are doing now, and mention that you have openings for clients. Explain some of the benefits to them of hiring a personal concierge, and give them business cards to hand out to their contacts as well.

If you have a "past life" in a previous career, go back to your old place of work and chat some people up there too. Always have a few business cards in your wallet, and a 30-second speech prepared to tell people what you do, which leads into finding prospects for clients.

When's it's time to stretch beyond the people you already know, start by thinking about your ideal client or target market, who they interact with on a daily basis, and where you think they spend their time. Following are some suggestions for places to start networking. Any of these routes could be helpful in locating clients. You can realistically target individual clients in this business because one person can generate a large percentage of your business.

It's impossible to give you a foolproof list as every market is different, so try out a few options to find what works for you:

- Attending or having a booth at tradeshows and public expos

- Joining service clubs or merchant associations (e.g., Kiwanis or Chamber of Commerce)

- Replying to "domestic help wanted" ads with a pitch for your service

- Approaching spouse groups of celebrities or athletes

- Joining community associations

- Contacting PR or management agencies and asking for referrals to their clients

- Approaching businesses whose employees work notoriously long hours or shift work

Joining Organizations

Local organizations can offer wonderful opportunities to network and establish contacts.

Networking Clubs

A valuable form of networking is through a networking club. Some of these are general business groups, but many have a target group of clients and include one member from different industries (e.g. insurance, financial planning, law, professional photography, real estate, etc.) to reach those in the target group. Each member of the club is expected to bring a certain number of leads to the group each week or month.

Fees will vary but can be as low as the cost of breakfast once a week or breakfast plus a membership fee. You may also be required to serve on the executive board after a time. In addition to the marketing opportunities, benefits of joining networking groups may include discounts on services provided by other members of the group.

To become a member you are either recommended to the group by an existing member, or you might approach the group and ask to sit in as an observer for a meeting or two, and get accepted from there. Most groups will allow a trial period before asking that you join or stop coming to meetings. You may be asked to give a short presentation about your own business, and on what business and personal skills you can bring to the group.

The types of participants will differ with every group, so don't settle for the first one you visit. Check around first before deciding which one to join. Make sure the members represent the kind of very busy people with reasonable incomes who might become clients for you, or who would know others who could benefit from your services.

One way to find a networking club is through word of mouth. You can also look for networking groups online. Business Network International (**www.bni.com**) has more than 2,300 chapters in cities around the world.

Membership Organizations

In addition to networking clubs, consider joining or attending events organized by groups that members of your target market belong to. For example, if you want to market to singles, get involved with singles organizations. If you want to work with women in business consider joining the National Association for Female Executives. Learn more about them at **www.nafe.com**.

Joining your local Chamber of Commerce is also a good idea. Your local Chamber will host various social and business-related meetings where you can meet a great variety of people, and get some great business advice besides. To find your local U.S. Chamber of Commerce visit **www. chamberofcommerce.com** or in Canada go to **www.chamber.ca/index. php/en/links/C57**.

Service Clubs

International service clubs like the Rotary Club (**www.rotary.org**), Kiwanis (**www.kiwanis.org**), or Lions Clubs (**www.lionsclubs.org**) are also good starting points. Joining service clubs is a great way to network and you'll meet people from all walks of life you can discuss your service offerings with. This can also help you gauge the demand for the services you plan to offer as well as help you to refine your target market.

Effective Networking

One of the first questions people ask when they meet is "What do you do?" When you respond, "I'm a personal concierge," most of them will ask you what that is. You have a perfect opening. Here's a sample you can use or adapt for your business:

> "I run a personal concierge service, and I help busy professionals rediscover their spare time. You know how it is — no one has time to get the car's oil changed, to grocery shop, run errands, or even to get organized. I personally take these and all sorts of tasks off people's plates,

so they can spend time doing what's really important, like relaxing with their family. I bet you could think of a few people you know who could use my help."

Also take an interest in the other members of any group you join. If you join a group with the intention of simply trying to cull as many business leads for yourself as possible, you probably won't be too popular.

To make the most out of your membership in an organization, there are several things you can do to raise your profile, including:

- Serve on a committee

- Write articles for the association newsletter

- Offer to give presentations on topics of interest to the members

- Do volunteer work that will bring you into contact with other members

- Run for election to the Executive Committee

Although networking and meeting as many people as possible are paramount, don't spread yourself too thin by joining more groups than you can possibly handle. Between attending meetings regularly and paying membership dues, becoming involved with too many groups can become a burden on your time and money.

Following Up

If you meet someone who seems genuinely interested in your services and you exchange business cards, don't stand on ceremony waiting for the person to call you. If you don't hear anything in a week, call him or her.

If you're targeting wealthy people, attend auctions, charity events, and grand openings. The newspaper's People or Society column often has a recap of events attended. Get involved with the arts (ballet, theater, symphony, opera, etc.) See if you qualify for membership in the local country club or private golf club, or spend the day at the spa. (If you don't have the cash to pursue these options, approach their management instead about partnership programs.)

When you target specific busy people, try to offer several weeks to sample your service and show them how they can benefit from being a regular client. When you approach service clubs or groups, offer to make a brief presentation about what a personal concierge does.

"I joined a couple of Chambers of Commerce and as a result, I got another Chamber member as my first client. She just had foot surgery and had a hard time getting to the store. Following her, the HR manager of the store I worked at used me to care for her five dogs while she was out of town. Both of those clients turned into regulars," says Jill Burstein of Jill will... Concierge Service.

"The most effective marketing tool for me has been networking and building relationships within different networking groups; which in turn create a great avenue for referrals and word of mouth advertising. The more you talk to everyone you meet about your business and the services you offer, the greater the opportunity to generate new business," adds Delmar Johnson of The Concierge Place.

Remember that people have extensive webs of contacts, so not all networking will land you a client on the spot. Not everyone you talk to will have a need for your services, but it's guaranteed that they know someone who does.

6.5.2   The Art of Self-Promotion

Most people who sell hate thinking of themselves as salespeople, but it's dangerous to neglect this part of your business. You don't have to be heavy-handed in your approach, but keep in mind that everyone you meet is a potential client. Every time you tell someone about your business, think of yourself as doing them a favor. If you believe in the value of the service you are offering, selling it to people becomes so much easier.

Expect that most people you meet will have no idea what a personal concierge does, and capitalize on that. Share a few stories (leaving out clients' names, of course) about some unusual requests or busy days you've had, and express how much you love what you do. Turn people on to the idea, and look for ways that your service could personally benefit them.

When you are first starting your business, you may find that offering a consultation and a few hours of free service to people is the best way to convince them to give you a try. Time is an intangible thing to try to sell, so any way you can demonstrate hands-on will help you out. Add their names (with their permission) into your database, so you can keep in touch with them after the few hours of service are used up.

You should also develop a follow-up letter you can send to clients who expressed interest in your service when you met them, but were not convinced on the spot. It can reiterate what a personal concierge does, and lets you give them some time to think about where your services are needed in their lives. Personalize the letter as much as you can. Then you can follow up the letter with a phone call in a few days to see if you can arrange a meeting.

"The most challenging part of running a business for me is acquiring new clients. It's been a challenge to build up clientele quickly, but I'm beginning to see the fruits of networking and talking about what I do," says Delmar Johnson of The Concierge Place.

In addition to landing new clients, self-promotion includes selling additional services to existing clients. As mentioned earlier, creative packages can sell services your clients may not have thought of. An e-newsletter sent a few times a year advising people of seasonal needs and packages is a nice, non-intrusive way to keep in touch.

Or you can arrange some kind of frequent communication that promotes your services at the same time — for example, an entertainment update that lets clients know of events and days tickets go on sale. A phone call every now and then is also a good way to remind them of you — just make sure you always ask if it's a good time to talk, so you don't become another drain on their time.

6.6 Marketing to Corporate Clients

The corporate world is increasingly embracing personal concierge services as a way to reward employees and attract clients. Employers are realizing that reducing undesirable personal commitments is more effective for increasing productivity than more pay. And condominiums, private clubs, gyms, and other businesses with membership or owner-ship to sell are also recognizing the cachet of adding personal concierge services to their list of benefits.

"Right now I have two corporations that pay me to run errands for their employees and their companies," says Jill Burstein of Jill will... Concierge Service. "There is a real need, and the idea is catching on. Everybody else starts looking bad if they don't offer a concierge service, like they don't care about their employees. Besides that, it's smart and economical to have a service when companies are cutting back on other benefits," she adds.

Working with corporate clients can be fun, exciting, and financially re-warding. The challenge will be deciding how much you can take on, and refining your approach for large groups. Some personal concierges prefer to build their business first with private clients before they tackle corporate, but it all depends on what you feel ready for. Here are some strategies you can use to enter into the corporate market.

6.6.1   Where to Find Corporate Clients

Which businesses are ready for corporate concierge service for their employees? Those that are successful, progressive, and committed to rewarding their employees. To find good candidates, check the busi-ness section of your local newspaper for profiles of successful compa-nies, notices of expansion, etc.

In general, you should be aware of who the big employers are in your area. For more detailed information about companies in your commu-nity, you can call your local Chamber of Commerce to get a list of their members.

Businesses that may be interested in offering concierge services as a value-addition to their primary service are generally those that cater to the wealthy, or that operate in very competitive conditions where they need a way to stand out from the competition.

You can approach:

- Bed and breakfasts

- Car dealerships

- Condo, apartment and office building developers

- Condo, apartment and office building management services

- Country clubs

- Cruise lines

- Golf courses

- Homebuilders

- Hotels

- Private hospitals

- Real estate agencies

- Seniors residences

- Spas

- Travel tour companies

It will be much easier to get a meeting arranged if you have a personal contact within the corporation or business. Even if the connection is tenuous, mention it when you make contact with the decision-maker.

6.6.2   How to Approach Corporate Clients

Once you've decided on the companies you want to approach about your services, you'll need to identify the best person to speak with, known as the decision-maker. Depending on the size of the company, that could be the owner, the CEO, the human resources manager, the sales manager, the president, or the head of the marketing department.

If you are unsure who to approach, explain a bit about what you do to the person who answers the phone, and ask for a recommendation. If you're still in doubt, you can contact several people within the organization and see where you get the best response. Most corporate entities also have a website, so you can check that out for more information on the company's operations and an "About Us" page, which might include contact information for its executive team.

Draft a brief letter of introduction to the decision-maker you've identified, which outlines some of the benefits of a personal concierge service for employees or as a value addition. You can use statistics about productivity and work/life balance as proof points. Include testimonials from some of your past or current clients. You might include clipped articles about other businesses that offer personal concierge services to their clients or employees.

You can call in advance of sending this letter to introduce yourself, and you will call after you send it to follow up. When you call, ask if they had any questions about your service, and what might be a good time to set up a meeting to tell them more about what you do.

If the response is, "We don't have a need for this type of service right now," you can counter with: "I understand how you feel. Many of my clients felt exactly the same way until I was able to show them how they could benefit from this service. I'd like to show you the same thing.

Would Monday or Tuesday be better for you?" If the response is still negative, you can move on to the next prospect on your list.

Above all, your focus should be on the value that you can add to the company. Statements like "I am a great shopper" or "I have five years worth of experience in booking airline tickets" tell them what you do, but not how they can benefit from your services. Instead, tell them "I have contacts throughout the retail and wholesale sectors and can get you excellent discounts on a variety of products I purchase for you" or "I have access to a huge number of business services that your company might not even be aware of, including reduced air fares." Statements like these will make the decision-maker start thinking about the money they can save and extra benefits they can realize from using your services.

6.7 Requests for Proposals

In some cases a corporate client will actively solicit proposals by advertising in a business publication or by contacting businesses that have come to their attention through networking, the Yellow Pages, online, etc. This process is called a Request for Proposal, or RFP. If a company is interested in hiring you, they may expect you to draft a written proposal of what you can offer them in terms of service and price. When you submit your proposal, you are making a "bid" to do the work.

6.7.1 Why Organizations Ask for Proposals

Sometimes the request for a proposal may come "out of the blue" from an employer you haven't approached. The beginning entrepreneur typically thinks this is great news. After all, why would they ask for a proposal if they were not interested in working with your company? Actually, there are a number of reasons employers ask for proposals:

It May Be Necessary for the Job

In some cases, a proposal is necessary for the job. They may want to compare your proposal with others they have received, or they may need to take your proposal to a higher level of decision-making. Many government departments require the decision-maker to review written proposals from several different prospects before a contract is awarded.

They will often have formal RFP guidelines such as those discussed above for you to follow. Likewise, some large companies require written proposals following strict submission guidelines.

If you pay attention to how they communicate with you, you should get a sense of how your proposal will be treated when it is received. Are they encouraging? Do they return your calls promptly? Do they sound positive about your chances? If the answer is "yes" and you want the job, then submitting a proposal is probably worth your time and energy.

It May Be a "Brush Off"

Some clients find it difficult to say "no" and want to avoid a confrontation. They can delay saying no by having you submit a proposal. The client can then say it is "under review" until you either give up or they finally work up the courage to tell you they are not interested.

It May Be Used to Confirm a Hiring Decision

The most common reason some types of clients ask for proposals is because they want to have written comparisons of several service providers. Often, they have a "preferred" company they want to hire, and the purpose of the written proposal is to help them confirm their decision, or show their supervisor or a hiring committee that they have "shopped around."

> **TIP:** If you are the preferred candidate you will know it. The client will have discussed the project with you in detail, and you will have reached a tentative agreement to do the work. They will explain that their regulations require them to review written proposals and may even assure you that it will be "just a formality."

If you are the preferred service provider and you want the job, then it is worth your time to put together a proposal confirming the details you have discussed with the clients. Otherwise, your time might be better spent focusing on clients who are seriously interested in you.

6.7.2   Responding to RFPs

If the client has a formal request for proposal process for bidders to follow, you will use that as the guideline in preparing your own response to the proposal. When you submit your proposal, you are making a "bid" to do the work, competing against other companies who also may be responding to the client's RFP.

The bid process may also require you to make an oral presentation. The organization requesting the RFP will usually hold a session (sometimes called a bidding meeting) for interested parties to attend in order to learn more about the project before submitting their response to the RFP. This is the time to ask questions and elicit clear answers. The more clearly you understand the goals and purpose of the project, the better your chances of being the successful bidder.

When responding to an RFP, make sure your response is submitted before the stated deadline and answers all of the questions accurately. Keep a current personal or company resume on file for these occasions, and don't overstate your qualifications to win a bid.

The client may not be obligated to award the contract to the lowest cost bidder. Instead, they may make their decision based on a number of factors, including the company's previous experience with similar projects.

If this sounds like a lot of work to get a job, it is. But keep in mind that the payoffs for a project like this are usually much greater than if you are working for an individual client. There are some other things to consider before you decide to respond to a corporation's request for proposal, though.

What to Include in an RFP

A proposal can be as simple as a one- or two-page summary of things you discussed in your meeting with the client, outlining the details of services you will provide (see the sample below). This may vary from regularly scheduled service for the entire office on certain days of the week, to you being on call for a key group of employees. If the company is not sure of the exact services they want, you can put together a few basic packages for them to choose from.

Include written references from past clients—even where you provided a service for free—and include a list of qualifications. Advise them of your availability and make certain you point out exactly how you will meet their objectives and what services are not within the scope of your contract.

Since you may not present your proposal in person, you should include written references from past clients with your proposal, and a biography outlining your qualifications to provide this service. You can reiterate the benefits you will bring to employees or clients, and to the company.

Sample Proposal of Services
For XYZ Corporation

Thank you for allowing Fabulous Concierge to prepare an outline of the service agreement we believe will suit the current needs of XYZ Corporation. We are happy to present the following:

Service Start Date:

August 1, 2013

Description of Services:

Fabulous Concierge will provide the following to XYZ Corporation:

- *Premier Service Level:* Provided to 3 (three) executives specified by XYZ Corporation. Includes up to 10 hours of any concierge service needed per week, per executive; minimum 1 hour booking.

- *Basic Service Package:* Provided to 12 (twelve) employees specified by XYZ Corporation. Includes dry cleaning pickup and drop off, errand services, reservation services, and gift purchasing only. To a maximum of 20 hours per month, per employee; minimum 1 hour booking.

Pricing:

- Basic Retainer: $30/mo per person (15) = $450 per month

- Executive hours billed at $30/hr, $1,000 maximum charge per month

- Hourly rate of $30/hr, $7,000 maximum charge per month

Terms:

Retainer of $450 and monthly prepayment of $2,000 required on the first of each month to cover upfront costs. Fabulous Concierge will provide detailed monthly records of time usage and prepayment balance at the end of each month, and will return any prepayment balance to XYZ Corporation that exceeds $5,000.

About Fabulous Concierge:

Started in 2006, this personalized service is run by Connie Concierge, a former nurse who knows what attending to people's personal needs quickly and professionally is all about. Other FC clients include ABC Corporation, ZZZ Widgets Inc., and many individual clients. See attached clips of FC coverage in local media.

References:

We encourage you to contact the following individuals, who have agreed to speak with you about how Fabulous Concierge is improving productivity and helping business thrive:

- Alan ABC
  HR Director, ABC Corporation
  (123) 555-1234

- Zelda ZZZ
  CEO, ZZZ Widgets Inc.
  (123) 555-4321

Fabulous Concierge is looking forward to meeting the needs of XYZ Corporation. Please contact Connie Concierge if you have any questions about this proposal or FC's services at (123) 555-1111. We will follow up with XYZ Corporation on this proposal in one week from today. Pricing listed is valid from 30 days of XYZ receiving this proposal.

You'll also need to specify any maximums on employee usage of your time, how employees or clients will contribute to your fees (if at all), and the method and frequency that the company will pay you. If there are obligations or exclusions either party has agreed to, they should be laid out as well. Refer back to section 5.1.3 on contracts for more details.

You can't assume that getting the go-ahead to write a proposal means you've landed the contract — but it means you're getting close. Writing a proposal can be time-consuming, but a great proposal can clinch a major client who can send your business skyrocketing, and take you to your next level of success.

Creating a Winning Proposal

If the client has not given you any formal guidelines you can still put together a winning proposal following the outline of RFP components listed earlier in this section. Be sure to include:

- A description of your company

- A description of the qualifications you will bring to the project and how those fit into the client's objectives

- A description of how you will meet the needs of the project and how those will benefit the client

- A description of fees and the hours you will work during the project

- References from other organizations for whom you have done similar projects

On the previous pages you will find a sample proposal that includes all of the elements listed above.

Formal RFPs

As mentioned above, an RFP is a written statement of the client's specific needs and information about the client's organization. In some cases, a company might require a more detailed and formal RFP. In this case, they will specify exactly the kind of information they require about you and the services to be provided, as well as the format they expect you to use in your response. The RFP outlines in detail what the client's project entails and why they want to hire a personal concierge service; what they expect in the project proposals received from such outside consultants; and the kinds of expertise required.

RFPs from corporations typically will offer an overview of the company and its business structure, some background on the planned project/event/services required, how and where to submit your proposal, how the proposal should be formatted, and what specific papers, documents and other submissions need to be included. It will also include the project's proposed budget, time frame, and any other conditions the project is subject to, as well as eligibility requirements for those wishing to submit a proposal, including the client's selection process and hiring criteria.

Here is an example of the type of information expected in a proposal:

- A description of your company

- Demonstration of your capability to develop and deliver the program

- Detailed description of the approach you will take in delivering the services

- A proposed timetable

- A fixed price quotation for development and delivery of the services

- Specific resources that you will assign to the project

- References from organizations you've provided similar services for

RFPs usually will include the following sections:

Introduction

The introduction often includes an overview of the organization and its organizational structure, a brief summary of the project and how it fits into the client's overall business objectives, a summary of the specific objectives for the project or event being considered, details of the project/event budget, and an explanation of why the client believes the services of an outside service provider are required.

Scope of Work/Services

This section details the work the client needs the service provider to perform. The scope of work or services obviously will vary from project to project and will be within your own area(s) of expertise for the most part or you wouldn't be considering responding to it. The client will outline exactly what services or work you are expected to provide for the project and may specify in this section any reports on performance and progress (i.e. how you are meeting the objectives) required during and at the end of the project. The client may also request from you in this section any specific background documentation regarding your qualifications for performing the work or services required by the project.

Contract Deliverables

During the course of the work being performed you may be required to submit certain plans, reports and other documents analyzing and detailing project planning, implementation, identification of any issues affecting the services provided and a detailed outline of cost allocations for the project as each stage is implemented. This section will detail what those requirements are.

Proposal Instructions

This section details the format for your proposal submission and what you must include in your proposal package. The client will specify where and to whom you will submit your proposal, and the format of any documents you provide. This may include seemingly trivial things like the maximum length of documents and line spacing (e.g. 15 single-spaced pages).

Proposal instructions may include other specifics about various forms, reports and other documents to be provided. Some examples are:

- *Technical Proposals:* Detailing logistics, identification of issues, draft work plans, etc.

- *Management Proposals:* Including who will do the work, how the work will be organized and managed, and the relevant experience of participants

- *Budget/Cost Proposals:* How the project budget will be allocated including labor and other expenses, identification of staff and the work they will do including their rates of pay, a breakdown of costs per project objective, etc.

- *Human Resources Proposals:* Labor and related issues such as time and costs, expertise specifics, details about any partner(s) and ancillary staff you will be bringing with you, etc.

- Any documents requiring signatures

To see some examples of RFPs you can check out the American Planning Association's website (**www.planning.org/consultants/request search.htm**), which maintains a list of RFPs for government and other contracts. For more information on how clients choose outside consultants, see "Choosing the Right Business Consultant, Business Trainer or Business Coach" at **http://sbinfocanada.about.com/cs/management/a/choosetrainer.htm**.

A number of companies specialize in writing proposals. You can find them by doing a web search for "writing proposals" and "contract." An excellent resource is the ProposalWriter.com website with links to proposal writing and government contracting. You may also find the book *Proven Proposal Strategies to Win More Business*, by Herman Holtz, helpful.

7. Conclusion

You are near the end of the *FabJob Guide to Become a Personal Concierge*. Hopefully, this is a new beginning as well — of your fabulous and successful career helping people live better lives, by taking away tasks they no longer have time for and giving them back their free time.

You need to remember three important things to be successful in this business; tenets which have been present throughout the information presented in this guide. They can be summarized using the acronym ACE:

Anticipate clients' needs before they happen.

Create new ways to serve your clients.

Exceed client expectations every time.

"Be realistic about how long it will take to build the business. And love to serve others!" advises Bev Riggins of Midwest Concierge Service. Personal concierge Delmar Johnson adds: "Being a personal concierge comes with a lot of variety, and can be very rewarding when you begin to find your footing. I would tell future concierges to remember the following:

- Customer service is the name of the game in this business.

- Develop relationships with other concierges who will have a wealth of knowledge to share.

- Identify your target market, and network with the people who can put you in contact with your potential clients.

- Don't get discouraged — being successful in this business does not happen overnight.

- Become a member of a concierge organization, and attend conferences and/or training.

- Most of all, don't to forget to have FUN with it!"

Personal concierge Dustyn Shroff offers, "there is no right or wrong way to approach this business, but the one thing that has always and will always remain a constant is that client satisfaction lies at the core of everything we do. Aim to be great at what you do, surpass expectations each step of the way, but always remember to remain grounded, humble and personable."

"If being a personal concierge is in your heart, it's in your future," concludes Jill Burstein of Jill will... Concierge Service. "Stop talking about it and just do it. I get people coming up to me all the time saying, 'My sister and I were going to do that. We've been talking about it for years!' I got sick of hearing myself talk about starting this business, so I finally did it."

Good luck to you!

Save 50% on Your Next Purchase

Please visit **www.FabJob.com/feedback.asp** to tell us how this guide has helped prepare you for your dream career. If we publish your comments, we will send you a gift certificate for 50% off your next purchase of a FabJob guide.

Get Free Career Advice

Get valuable career advice for free by subscribing to the FabJob newsletter. You'll receive insightful tips on: how to break into the job of your dreams or start the business of your dreams. You'll also receive discounts on FabJob guides. Subscribe to the FabJob newsletter at **www.FabJob.com/newsletter.asp**.

Join FabJob on Facebook

Go to **www.facebook.com/FabJob** and click the "Like" button to be among the first to get FabJob news and special offers.

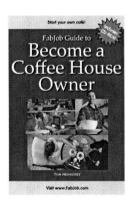
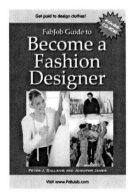

Does Someone You Love Deserve a Dream Career?

Giving a FabJob® guide is a fabulous way to show someone you believe in them and support their dreams. Help them break into the career of their dreams with more than 75 career guides to choose from.

Visit www.FabJob.com to order guides today!

More Guides to Build Your Business

Increase your income by offering additional services. Here are some recommended FabJob guides to help you build your business:

Get Paid to Shop

Imagine having a creative high-paying job shopping for fashions, housewares, gifts, or almost anything else you love to shop for. In the **FabJob Guide to Become a Personal Shopper** you will discover:

- Step-by-step instructions for personal shopping from identifying what people want to finding the best products and retailers

- How to get discounts on merchandise

- How to prevent purchasing mistakes

- How to get a job as a personal shopper for a boutique, department store or shopping center

- How to start a personal shopping business, price your services, and find clients

Get Paid to Organize

As a professional organizer you can use your creativity to help people, homes and offices get organized. In the **FabJob Guide to Become a Professional Organizer** you will receive:

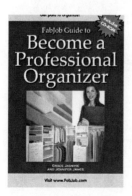

- A room-by-room guide to home organizing and reducing clutter

- Valuable information on how to organize businesses including managing workflow, filing systems, and space planning

- Personal organization and time management tips

- Advice to help you start a professional organizing businesses, set your prices, and attract customers

Visit www.FabJob.com to order guides today!

How to Install the CD-ROM

The bonus CD-ROM found at the end of this book contains helpful forms and checklists you can revise and use in your own business. It also includes an electronic version of this book, which you can use to quickly connect to the websites we've mentioned (as long as you have access to the Internet and the Acrobat Reader program on your computer).

To install the CD-ROM, these simple steps will work with most computers:

1. Insert the CD-ROM into your computer CD drive.

2. Double click on the "My Computer" icon (PC) or the "Finder" icon (Mac) on your desktop.

3. Double click on the icon for your CD-ROM drive.

4. Read the "Read Me" file on the CD-ROM for more information.

CPSIA information can be obtained at www.ICGtesting.com
Printed in the USA
BVOW0120 119 112

305969BV   5B/2 P